NO LONGER QUIET

A Citizen's Guide to Protecting Our Democracy

D.C. Burnette

El Burno Publishing

While every effort has been made to cite all sources appropriately, some concepts and ideas may be attributed to previous works without explicit citation. The intent is not to plagiarize, but to acknowledge the breadth of the conversation and the collective contributions of researchers and thinkers in this field.

Published by El Burno Publishing, an imprint of El Burno Productions, Ltd.
Fort Collins, Colorado 2025
www.elburno.com

ISBNs:
Hard Cover: 978-1-967976-04-1
Paperback: 978-1-967976-05-8
Ebook: 978-1-967976-06-5

Printed in the United States of America

For permission requests, contact: elburnoproductions@gmail.com

Dedicated to those who keep watch while the rest of us sleep, challenge what's wrong, protect what's right, and remember what matters.

Acknowledgments

This book would not exist without the unshakable support and wisdom of my family, my friends, and my colleagues. Your clarity, conviction, and care are on every page.

Deep gratitude to the public servants - past and present - who inspired these words through their integrity, resilience, and quiet acts of resistance.

Thank you to the educators, librarians, and civic leaders who continue to light the path in dark times.

Special thanks to the dedicated staff at my publisher, El Burno Publishing, who reviewed early drafts, provided guidance and direction, asked hard questions, and helped sharpen the arguments. Your candor made the work better.

And finally, to every reader committed to understanding and defending democracy, you are the reason this book was written.

-D.C. Burnette

"Eternal vigilance is the price of liberty."

THOMAS JEFFERSON

PUBLISHER'S NOTE

On the Origins of This Work

This book was written entirely by sentient hands, shaped by lived experience, academic study, and years of public service. No content in this volume was generated by artificial intelligence.

The observations, arguments, and insights found in these pages are the product of a deeply personal concern for the health of American democracy, drawn from disciplines as varied as history, law, literature, and civic education. Every quote has been read, every case studied, every example chosen for its relevance—not assembled by algorithm, but curated through reflection and intent.

While we acknowledge that technology plays a role in modern publishing—just as it does in communication, design, and editing— this manuscript reflects the full attention of its author. It is a labor of memory, conscience, and democratic faith.

D.C. Burnette, the author, is committed to civic renewal and public literacy. Their work—through El Burno Publishing—seeks to illuminate, not automate; to empower, not replace. This book is part of that mission.

— *El Burno Publishing, April 2025.*

CONTENTS

INTRODUCTION

The Cost of Complacency

"A popular government without popular information or the means of acquiring it is but a prologue to a farce or a tragedy." — James Madison, Letter to W. T. Barry, August 4, 1822

In the early days of the American experiment, the Founders worried not about conquest from foreign enemies, but about a quieter, more insidious threat: the slow death of democracy from within. The fear was that liberty would not be stolen at gunpoint, but surrendered by a citizenry too distracted, too uninformed, or too indifferent to notice.

Their concern was not paranoia, it was historical wisdom. They had studied the fall of Athens, the decay of the Roman Republic, and the slow descent of Enlightenment Europe into authoritarianism. They understood that the real threat to liberty comes not from external attack, but from the internal erosion of civic virtue, public education, and shared commitment to reason and justice. They knew that a republic could collapse not from a dramatic overthrow, but from the daily neglect of its foundations.

They were right to worry.

> "I saw the best minds of my generation destroyed by madness, starving hysterical naked..." — Allen Ginsberg, *Howl*, 1956

Ginsberg's haunting observation captures the spiritual and intellectual collapse that occurs when a society ceases to care, to question, or to think critically, a warning that foreshadows the slow civic decay described in the pages ahead.

Today, across the globe and within our own communities, democratic institutions are under siege, not by revolutionaries, but by the subtle corrosion of civic ignorance, institutional decay, disinformation, and a public that has, in many places, simply stopped paying attention. Once-thriving republics are sliding into authoritarianism not with a bang, but with a shrug.

This book is about that shrug.

It is about the slow unraveling of democratic systems in the absence of an engaged, educated, and courageous public. It is also about the voices—ancient and modern, literary and political—that saw this coming. From Aristotle to Orwell, from Tocqueville to Angela Davis, the message is clear: democracy is not a machine that runs on autopilot. It demands maintenance. It demands participation. And most of all, it demands that citizens be taught, inspired, and equipped to guard it against both force and fraud.

We will explore this theme through a wide lens. Moving from ancient philosophy to dystopian fiction, from historical collapses to modern resistance, and ending with a study of those individuals who still uphold democratic ideals today. These chapters span political theory, literature, history, and institutional analysis. These works do not always agree on method, but they are united in their conclusion: **a democratic**

society that fails to educate its citizens is not a democracy for long.

This is not a nostalgic lament or abstract theoretical exercise. The warning signs are all around us: rising authoritarian populism, the global rollback of civil liberties, and the mass retreat into tribal identity over shared public reason. These are not isolated problems; they are symptoms of a deeper democratic crisis; one caused, in part, by the erosion of intellectual and civic engagement.

We must reckon with the fact that democracy is perishable. It does not die only in coups or on battlefields. Sometimes, it dies in living rooms, as citizens scroll endlessly past truth. Sometimes, it dies in classrooms, where critical thinking is treated as subversive. And sometimes, it dies at the ballot box, not because votes are stolen, but because minds are never made.

This book is not about despair. It is about vigilance. It is also about people, the lawyers, educators, public servants, whistleblowers, and ordinary citizens, whose everyday choices become the final safeguard when laws and institutions falter. In the pages that follow, we will listen to the voices that warned us and learn from the texts that tried to arm us against tyranny, whether in the form of a boot on the neck or a screen in the hand. By the end, we may rediscover what democracy truly requires, and what it will cost us if we don't rise to meet that obligation. Raise our voice and be quiet no longer.

CHAPTER ONE

The Ancient Warning —
Democracy Requires Virtue

"The fate of empires depends on the education of youth." —
Aristotle, attributed in various educational treatises reflecting
ancient Greek civic values

D emocracy, in its modern form, is often sold as a guarantee-
of rights, of freedoms, of equality before the law. But for
the ancient philosophers, democracy was not a promise; it
was a gamble. And it was a dangerous one.

The idea that a people could govern themselves was considered not
just radical. It was unstable, chaotic, even reckless. Why? Because it
presumed that the average citizen had both the *capacity* and the *will* to
prioritize the public good over private interest. The Greek philosophers
knew better. They saw what happened when masses ruled without
reason: democracy, untethered from virtue and education, slid easily
into demagoguery, factionalism, and eventually tyranny.

To understand how the United States interprets these ancient warnings,
we must also clarify what is meant by a 'republican form of
democracy.' In the American context, a republican democracy is not
a contradiction. It is a hybrid: a system where the people govern

through elected representatives, constrained by a constitution designed to limit the abuse of power and protect minority rights. Unlike pure direct democracy, where citizens vote on laws themselves, a republican democracy employs a system of representative government, with institutional checks and balances to safeguard against mob rule, tyranny of the majority, or authoritarian takeover. This structure assumes that public virtue must be supported not only by civic education but by the architecture of institutions—separation of powers, regular elections, a free press, and an independent judiciary.

The Founders drew from both classical theory and Enlightenment principles to engineer a government that could withstand human frailty and factionalism. They knew that unchecked democracy could collapse into demagoguery, just as unchecked authority could become despotism. The American experiment, therefore, is not simply democratic—it is a constitutional republic. And that distinction is not semantic. It is the framework that allows freedom to exist within the rule of law.

The Founders built a system meant to withstand time, but they knew even strong systems fail when their moral engine goes cold. Today, we face many of the same pressures they feared.

I. The Classical Vision of Civic Education

Aristotle insisted that democratic survival requires education in virtue. Without it, citizens cannot distinguish between liberty and license. In *Politics*, he emphasized that civic education should prepare citizens not just to earn a living, but to live nobly and contribute to the public life of the *polis*. A society that prioritizes utility over virtue, he warned, builds a foundation too weak to endure.

This principle was not merely theoretical. In classical Athens, civic education—*paideia*—was a structured and essential component of male citizenship. Young Athenian men were taught rhetoric, ethics, music, and physical education, all aimed at producing well-rounded citizens capable of deliberation and defense of the city-state. Yet Athens also serves as a cautionary tale: despite this investment in education, its democracy ultimately fell to demagoguery and imperial overreach. The trial and execution of Socrates in 399 BCE, a consequence of political scapegoating and anti-intellectual sentiment, exposed the fragility of democratic institutions when public reason is overtaken by fear and populism.

In contrast, the Roman Republic emphasized civic duty through its legal and military systems. Roman youth of the elite classes studied rhetoric, philosophy, and history under private tutors, with the goal of shaping orators and magistrates. Cicero, in particular, championed the idea that a republic could only survive with citizens educated in virtue and law. Yet Rome, too, succumbed to internal decay, civil wars, corruption, and concentration of power, showing that education without widespread civic engagement could not prevent republics from collapsing into empire. This pattern would repeat across history: without a robust and participatory civic culture, even the most sophisticated institutions rot from within.

Plato was even less optimistic. In *The Republic*, he mapped a descent from aristocracy to democracy to tyranny. His critique was rooted in a view that democracy, by promoting total equality without adequate cultivation of reason and virtue, inevitably dissolves into disorder. For Plato, a democracy gives birth to a culture where desires are unchecked, authority is distrusted, and every opinion—no matter how uninformed —is given equal weight. This, he argued, leads to a breakdown of shared standards and paves the way for a tyrant who promises order amidst the chaos.

> "The excess of liberty, whether in states or individuals, seems only to pass into excess of slavery." — Plato, *The Republic*, Book VIII

In Plato's account, democracy fails when citizens confuse freedom with entitlement. They reject expertise and elevate charisma over character. And in the resulting chaos, a tyrant rises, not by force, but by popular acclaim.

Aristotle, though more pragmatic than Plato, agreed that education in virtue was indispensable. In *Politics*, he outlined three kinds of good governance—monarchy, aristocracy, and polity—and warned that each had a corrupt counterpart: tyranny, oligarchy, and democracy in its degraded form. While he saw polity (a mixed constitutional system with broad participation) as the most stable, he emphasized that it could only survive if citizens were trained to rule and be ruled in turn. This reciprocal understanding of citizenship—rooted in rational discourse and public virtue—was, for Aristotle, the lifeblood of the state.

Where Plato feared democratic disorder, Aristotle sought to manage it through moral formation. His approach was not to reject democracy outright, but to elevate it through education. In this way, both thinkers converge on the same truth: liberty without wisdom becomes its own undoing.

II. Enlightenment Foundations of Liberty and Reason

Fast forward to John Stuart Mill, who in *On Liberty* offers democracy a robust defense, but with a critical caveat. Freedom, he argued, must be rooted in intellectual discipline and public discourse. Without space for dissent and diversity of thought, democratic societies decay into mediocrity and mob rule.

> "The worth of a state in the long run is the worth of the individuals composing it." — John Stuart Mill, *On Liberty*, 1859

Mill's vision of liberty demanded citizens capable of reasoned judgment —capable of listening, questioning, and resisting the tyranny of public opinion. He believed that genuine freedom required a contest of ideas, where truth emerged not by decree but through open debate and rigorous scrutiny. For Mill, the suppression of dissent, even if well-intentioned, was a grave threat to liberty, because it denied society the corrective power of criticism. He viewed education not simply as the transmission of facts, but as the cultivation of independent judgment and moral courage.

In his view, democracies that discouraged disagreement or tolerated intellectual laziness risked becoming majoritarian mobs rather than guardians of individual rights. The health of a democracy, he argued, depended on the extent to which its citizens could think freely, express unpopular opinions, and change their minds based on reason. Without these qualities, freedom would become hollow, and democratic institutions would rot from the inside.

This Enlightenment ideal took institutional form in educational reforms across Europe. The Prussian system of the early 19th century, for example, developed a national, compulsory education framework designed not only to promote literacy, but to foster civic order and duty. While later criticized for emphasizing obedience, the Prussian model influenced global education systems, particularly through its incorporation of structured teacher training, secular curriculum, and moral instruction.

In revolutionary France, the founding of the lycées under Napoleon in 1802 aimed to produce citizens capable of serving the Republic. These secondary schools provided a classical education in philosophy, rhetoric, and science, intended not just to prepare students for university, but to instill civic responsibility and national identity. Though the Napoleonic agenda was authoritarian in structure, the educational architecture reflected Enlightenment values about the role of education in shaping rational, capable citizens.

These case studies illustrate that the Enlightenment's legacy was not confined to ideas, it reshaped institutions. They laid the groundwork for modern civic systems that aim to cultivate reasoned debate, individual responsibility, and public virtue. And it proved that civic education is not an abstract virtue, but a practical necessity in the defense of democratic life.

III. The American Experiment: Fragile by Design

The American Founders were steeped in this tradition. James Madison, writing in *Federalist No. 10*, worried about factions and the erosion of the common good.

> "Liberty is to faction what air is to fire." — James Madison, *Federalist No. 10*, 1787

Madison believed that only a large, diverse republic could counteract factionalism, but only if its citizens were educated and discerning.

This belief in the foundational role of education in a republic was institutionalized early in the nation's history. The Northwest Ordinance of 1787, a landmark piece of legislation governing the expansion of the United States, declared that "Religion, morality, and knowledge being necessary to good government and the happiness of mankind, schools and the means of education shall forever be encouraged." This was more than aspirational language. It recognized that democratic governance required an educated public.

To fulfill that vision, early American reformers such as Noah Webster took up the task of building a civic culture through education. Webster's spellers and readers were designed not only to teach literacy, but to instill republican values. His textbooks emphasized unity, national identity, and moral virtue. Qualities he believed essential for self-governance.

> "The preservation of the sacred fire of liberty... is finally staked, on the experiment entrusted to the hands of the American people." — George Washington, *First Inaugural Address*, 1789

Washington's warning is more than a ceremonial flourish, it is a foundational truth. His quote underscores the Founders' belief that liberty was not self-sustaining, but rather a fragile trust passed from one generation to the next. By stating that the sacred fire of liberty is entrusted to the American people, Washington made clear that the republic's survival hinges not on its documents or leaders, but on the daily engagement of its citizens. Democracy cannot be preserved through sentiment or ceremony alone; it requires sustained participation and public virtue. Inserting ourselves into the life of the republic, through education, discourse, dissent, and principled service, is not optional. It is the only way to ensure that freedom endures.

George Washington, in his *Farewell Address*, reiterated and expanded upon the theme he introduced in his First Inaugural Address: that liberty is not guaranteed by structure alone, but by the vigilance of the people. His address was not merely a parting message, it was a constitutional supplement, meant to fortify the ethical underpinnings of the young republic. Washington emphasized that the diffusion of knowledge was essential to sustain public virtue and guard against the insidious pull of faction and despotism. He warned against the dangers of political factionalism, regional divisions, and entangling foreign alliances, all of which could undermine the republic if citizens lost sight of their shared identity and responsibilities. Central to his message was the conviction that a free government could not exist without informed and principled citizens. For Washington, education was not merely a private good, but a national imperative, necessary to cultivate public virtue, uphold unity, and ensure the survival of the union.

> "Promote, then, as an object of primary importance, institutions for the general diffusion of knowledge." — George Washington, *Farewell Address*, 1796

Abraham Lincoln echoed this theme in his *Lyceum Address*, warning that the real danger to the republic would come not from abroad, but from within. Delivered at the age of twenty-eight, Lincoln's speech condemned mob violence, lawlessness, and the corrosion of public institutions. He argued that America's greatest threat lay in the erosion of civic respect for law and democratic norms. For Lincoln, the preservation of liberty required a 'political religion', a national commitment to the Constitution, reasoned discourse, and legal restraint. He called on Americans to elevate their reverence for law above personal passions, knowing that the rot of a republic begins when its citizens lose faith in the civic process.

"If destruction be our lot, we must ourselves be its author and finisher." — Abraham Lincoln, *Lyceum Address*, 1838

These early efforts established a uniquely American expectation: that the survival of the republic depended on a literate, informed, and morally grounded public. As public schooling expanded across the 19th century, that civic mission was always part of its core purpose. The crisis today lies not in the abandonment of that idea, but in our collective failure to remember its urgency.

IV. Conclusion: Ancient Wisdom for a Modern Crisis

These classical and early modern thinkers did not place blind faith in the masses. They placed conditional faith—in a people *willing to educate themselves* and uphold virtue through daily civic engagement. For Aristotle, Plato, Mill, Madison, and Lincoln, the message is clear: democracy is not natural. It is not permanent. And it is not easy. It must be cultivated intentionally, defended vigorously, and taught across generations. Without an informed and morally grounded public, democratic systems inevitably decay. Succumbing not just to external threats, but to internal apathy, ignorance, and erosion of civic will.

It must be built, defended, and, most importantly, *taught*. The next chapter will turn to fiction, where authors like Orwell, Huxley, and Atwood carry these ancient and Enlightenment warnings into modern settings, portraying what happens when democratic cultures abandon civic memory and moral clarity. We turn next to the imagined futures of these writers, whose cautionary tales show what happens when vigilance gives way to apathy, and when freedom is surrendered without a fight.

CHAPTER TWO

The Literary Warnings —
Dystopias and Disengagement

*"The people will not revolt. They will not look up from their
screens long enough to notice what's happening." — George
Orwell, 1984, 1949*

I f the philosophers gave us the theoretical framework for
understanding democratic decay, it is the writers of dystopian
fiction who made it visceral. With chilling clarity, they
mapped the psychological, cultural, and technological conditions
that make people vulnerable to authoritarianism. They
understood that tyranny does not always arrive with the sound
of boots or the clatter of chains. It often comes quietly, under the
guise of convenience, entertainment, or even patriotism. These
authors foresaw the corrosive effects of a disengaged citizenry, a
distracted public, and an educational system that fails to foster
critical thinking. Their imagined futures were not just cautionary
tales. They were mirrors held up to societies losing the will to
remain free.

I. Orwell's World: Truth as a Casualty of Complacency

In *1984*, George Orwell offers a regime that maintains power not only through terror, but through the control of language and history. Citizens are bombarded with propaganda, trained to embrace contradictions, and numbed into passive compliance.

> "The people will not revolt. They will not look up from their screens long enough to notice what's happening."

Orwell warned us of a society in which truth itself is malleable, and education becomes indoctrination. In such a world, civic virtue dies not in a purge, but in a sigh. The most terrifying aspect of Orwell's dystopia is not the violence—it is the apathy of the populace, conditioned to accept lies as truth and to forget even the act of forgetting.

The totalitarian state in *1984* survives by erasing the past, inventing new enemies, and rewriting language through "Newspeak", a linguistic system designed to eliminate dissent by narrowing the range of thought itself. When citizens lack the vocabulary to express rebellion, the very idea of resistance becomes unthinkable. This concept is not fictional hyperbole; it has played out repeatedly in the 20th century. Stalinist Russia, for example, utilized show trials, purged historical records, and promoted a cult of personality that merged myth with governance. Nazi Germany wielded propaganda through education, film, and media to shape mass consciousness and eliminate alternative narratives.

Today, Orwell's warning echoes in more subtle forms: algorithmic echo chambers, disinformation campaigns, and political movements that normalize falsehoods by sheer repetition. The phrase "alternative facts," once the subject of satire, has become a feature of public discourse. When the boundary between truth and fiction is eroded, democracy is reduced to theater, and the citizen becomes a spectator, not a participant.

II. Bradbury's Burned Books: Voluntary Illiteracy and Entertainment Culture

Ray Bradbury's *Fahrenheit 451* envisions a society that no longer needs to ban books, because no one wants to read them. The fireman protagonist, Guy Montag, slowly awakens to a culture so inundated by noise, distraction, and shallow pleasure that depth and dissent are drowned out.

> "You don't have to burn books to destroy a culture. Just get people to stop reading them." — Ray Bradbury, Interview with *The Times*, October 1993

This vision resonates in an era dominated by algorithms, infotainment, and passive consumption. The threat is not state censorship but mass disinterest in truth, critical thought, and historical memory. In Bradbury's world, books represent not only knowledge but introspection. A quiet threat to a system built on emotional gratification and social conformity.

Bradbury's firemen do not hunt down political radicals, they incinerate the means of awakening. Schools cease teaching inquiry. Mass media drowns out nuance with noise. Apathy, not oppression, is the force behind the collapse of civic consciousness.

Historically, parallels can be found in both democratic and authoritarian societies. In 20th-century America, the rise of television shifted public focus from civic participation to passive entertainment. Political debates became media spectacles, and advertising supplanted deliberation. Meanwhile, in Francoist Spain, cultural policy promoted religious conformity and escapist cinema while suppressing dissenting views and minority languages. In both cases, public attention was steered away from critical thought toward distractions that dulled civic awareness. More recently, the emergence of social media echo chambers has intensified this condition, replacing thoughtful engagement with curated distraction and tribal confirmation.

Bradbury's dystopia warns us not just of state control, but of voluntary intellectual surrender. His message is clear: **when a society stops reading, it stops thinking, and when it stops thinking, it becomes ripe for control.**

III. Huxley's Comfort Trap: Sedated by Choice

> "Better to sleep in an uncomfortable bed free, than sleep in a comfortable bed unfree." — Jack Kerouac, *On the Road*, 1957

Kerouac's insight captures the soul of Huxley's warning: comfort without liberty is a gilded cage. In trading away discomfort, debate, and dissent, a society may gain calm, but lose the civic muscle required to stay free.

Aldous Huxley's *Brave New World* presents a subtler, more seductive tyranny. Here, the populace is kept in line not by force, but by pleasure, endless entertainment, sexual freedom, and the drug "soma."

> "A really efficient totalitarian state would be one in which the all-powerful executive... need not coerce because people love their servitude." — Aldous Huxley, *Brave New World Revisited*, 1958

Huxley's citizens are not oppressed, they are anesthetized. It's a warning that the erosion of democracy might not come with jackboots, but with a smile. The lesson: **a citizenry that chooses comfort over conscience loses both.**

What makes Huxley's warning so potent is that it reframes tyranny not as something imposed from above, but as something eagerly accepted. In *Brave New World*, people are conditioned from birth to avoid discomfort, dissent, and deep thought. Their allegiance is not demanded; it is manufactured through gratification. Science, literature, and philosophy are replaced with shallow slogans, synthetic happiness, and endless consumption.

This scenario finds echoes in the post-World War II consumer boom in the United States. Suburban prosperity, television, and advertising created a culture increasingly focused on comfort and leisure. At the same time, civic engagement declined, with voter turnout and union participation dropping. In the Soviet Union, limited material privileges were used strategically to co-opt compliance among the professional classes. Huxley's dystopia reminds us that when pleasure becomes the primary political pacifier, liberty erodes without resistance.

In today's attention economy, Huxley's concerns have metastasized. Endless scrolling, personalized algorithms, and instant gratification have created an environment where boredom is feared, silence is rare, and introspection is nearly obsolete. We risk becoming a society so sedated by entertainment that we no longer notice, or care, when power consolidates, freedoms vanish, or truth is manipulated.

IV. Atwood's Theocracy: Memory, Power, and Denial

Margaret Atwood's *The Handmaid's Tale* dramatizes how quickly a liberal democracy can collapse into theocratic authoritarianism when rights are stripped in the name of order and morality. The novel explores how oppression is made palatable through nostalgia and selective memory.

> "When we think of the past it's the beautiful things we pick out. We want to believe it was all like that." — Margaret Atwood, *The Handmaid's Tale*, 1985

This selective amnesia enables cruelty. Without an educated public to challenge false narratives, injustice becomes normalized. Atwood constructs a world where the past is edited, women's autonomy is erased, and the language of virtue is co-opted to legitimize hierarchy. Her protagonist, Offred, navigates a society where religious language is used to sacralize submission and where fear is internalized so deeply that resistance seems unimaginable.

Atwood's warnings reflect historical transformations. The rise of Iran's Islamic Republic after 1979 is a stark example, where democratic institutions were replaced by a clerical regime invoking divine authority. Similarly, during the American Reconstruction and Jim Crow eras, Southern states revised history to portray slavery as benign and the Confederacy as noble. Rewriting curricula and controlling textbooks to uphold a racial caste system. These efforts to reshape collective memory are not relics of the past; they are tactics still used by authoritarian movements to sanitize oppression and discourage resistance.

Theocratic regimes and authoritarian nostalgists both rely on myth-making. They do not need to suppress truth outright if they can replace it with a comforting lie. Atwood's dystopia is a cautionary tale about how easily liberal societies can fall into tyranny, not because they forget the past, but because they remember it wrongly, selectively, and sentimentally.

Where Atwood highlights theocratic control and weaponized memory, Sinclair Lewis offers a subtler warning; one rooted not in fear, but in fatigue.

V. Lewis's Lull: Mediocrity as a Mechanism of Control

In *It Can't Happen Here*, Sinclair Lewis imagines the rise of an American dictator. His path to power is not through violence, but through populism, nationalism, and the public's tolerance for mediocrity.

> "The tyranny of this dictatorship isn't going to be primarily the tyranny of hideous punishments. It's going to be the tyranny of boredom, of dullness, of all-around

mediocrity." — Sinclair Lewis, *It Can't Happen Here*, 1935

Lewis captures the danger of political disengagement and the slow normalization of authoritarian rule. His fictional character, Berzelius "Buzz" Windrip, is not a monster but a mediocrity; bombastic, banal, and embraced by a public too tired or indifferent to resist. The novel is a warning against the complacency that allows democratic norms to erode under the weight of spectacle and empty slogans.

His vision finds resonance in Fascist Italy under Mussolini, where populist rhetoric and the appeal to national pride eclipsed democratic norms. The regime was sustained not by mass terror, but by habituation to spectacle and indifference to political pluralism. In contemporary Venezuela, authoritarianism advanced through populist messaging and institutional erosion, accompanied by disillusionment among the electorate. In both contexts, the public's resignation to dysfunction proved more dangerous than outright repression.

Lewis understood that tyranny rarely begins with a declaration. It begins with a shrug. When a public loses interest in excellence, civic responsibility, and truth, it becomes susceptible to leadership that offers comfort over competence. His novel is less about how dictators rise and more about how democracies fall; not with a roar, but with a yawn.

VI. Conclusion: Fiction as Forewarning

These dystopian works are not merely speculative fiction. They are strategic warnings about how democracy fails when its citizens are no longer curious, no longer critical, and no longer committed to truth. Orwell warned of surveillance and propaganda. Bradbury and Huxley warned of seduction and distraction. Atwood and Lewis warned that democratic erosion can come wrapped in tradition, religion, and patriotism.

Each of these authors reminds us that **the collapse of democracy does not require a coup—it only requires a citizenry too distracted, too complacent, or too comfortable to care.**

Together, they reinforce a shared insight: education, literacy, historical awareness, and moral imagination are not luxuries. They are the scaffolding of a functioning democracy. Without them, the republic becomes hollow, vulnerable to authoritarian drift and societal amnesia.

Their warnings carry a final implication: fiction is not escape, it is rehearsal. These novels train us to see subtle threats before they harden into crisis.

The next chapter turns from fiction to fact, tracing real-world patterns of institutional erosion, and examining how the systems that support democracy begin to fracture from within.

CHAPTER THREE

History Speaks — Collapse
and Resistance

"The limits of tyrants are prescribed by the endurance of those whom they oppress." — Frederick Douglass, "What to the Slave Is the Fourth of July?" Speech, 1852

W hile fiction gives us vivid warnings of democratic collapse, history provides the proof. Across centuries and continents, once-vibrant republics and constitutional orders have withered; not because their enemies were too strong, but because their citizens became too passive. Democracies have crumbled not from a single catastrophic event, but from an accumulation of compromises, silences, and missed opportunities. The slow erosion of civic habits, the decay of public trust, the retreat from education and discourse. These are the harbingers of collapse.

History reminds us that the collapse of freedom is rarely dramatic. More often, it is procedural. Laws are amended, institutions are repurposed, norms are quietly ignored, and dissent is dismissed as disloyalty. When the population is no longer taught to question, no longer encouraged to participate, and no longer capable of distinguishing truth from ideology, authoritarianism fills the void.

This chapter turns to the real-world examples that demonstrate these patterns. From Nazi Germany to contemporary Venezuela, from the civil rights movement to modern acts of resistance, the record speaks clearly: the failure of democratic institutions begins with the failure of democratic citizenship.

I. Arendt's Diagnosis: The Death of Truth

In *The Origins of Totalitarianism*, Hannah Arendt described how modern tyrannies emerge not only through violence, but through the destruction of truth itself.

> "The ideal subject of totalitarian rule is not the convinced Nazi or the convinced Communist, but people for whom the distinction between fact and fiction... no longer exists." — Hannah Arendt, *The Origins of Totalitarianism*, 1951

Arendt's insight is more relevant now than ever. In an age of misinformation and digital propaganda, the blurring of fact and fiction destabilizes public judgment. When citizens no longer trust institutions, journalism, or even shared reality, they become pliable, open to the strongest voice, not the most truthful one.

Arendt argued that totalitarian regimes depend not on belief, but on confusion. When everything becomes suspect and no authority is seen as credible, citizens become paralyzed. In such a world, propaganda is not meant to persuade; it is meant to exhaust. The goal is not to replace truth with lies, but to create a landscape where truth no longer matters.

Historically, this phenomenon played out in Nazi Germany, where the Ministry of Propaganda controlled information through mass media, education, and censorship. Citizens were inundated with ideology masked as truth, and dissenting voices were systematically silenced. The Soviet Union under Stalin also perfected the suppression of truth: photographs were altered, historical records falsified, and political opponents "disappeared" from public memory. These regimes demonstrated how the destruction of truth forms the bedrock of authoritarian power.

In today's media ecosystem, these lessons echo ominously. The proliferation of conspiracy theories, partisan news silos, and "alternative facts" threatens the foundations of democratic discourse. Algorithms amplify outrage, while deepfakes and disinformation campaigns muddy the waters of public understanding. When truth becomes subjective, civic dialogue collapses and with it, the capacity for collective action.

Arendt warned that this decay begins not with state censorship, but with cultural surrender: when people grow weary of complexity and choose comfort over clarity. Her work stands as a reminder that democracy relies not just on elections and institutions, but on a shared commitment to truth as a common good.

II. Democratic Erosion in Real Time

Steven Levitsky and Daniel Ziblatt, in *How Democracies Die*, show that democratic collapse is rarely sudden. It unfolds slowly, in "barely visible steps," through legal loopholes, weakened norms, and complicit elites.

> "Democracies erode slowly, in barely visible steps." — Steven Levitsky and Daniel Ziblatt, *How Democracies Die*, 2018

Their work warns against the false comfort that democratic institutions, once established, will defend themselves. They demonstrate how constitutional forms, such as elections, courts, and legislatures, can remain intact even as their functions are hollowed out. Leaders do not need to abolish the rule of law to destroy it; they only need to bend it to serve power rather than the people.

They cite examples from Venezuela, Turkey, Hungary, and even the United States, illustrating how leaders consolidate power while keeping the appearance of legality. A disengaged or polarized public often fails to resist until it is too late.

Hungary's Viktor Orbán has used democratic elections to entrench illiberal governance, systematically dismantling judicial independence, media pluralism, and civil society. In Turkey, President Erdoğan has leveraged constitutional referendums and emergency decrees to weaken checks and balances, suppress dissent, and centralize power. In Venezuela, Hugo Chávez and later Nicolás Maduro hollowed out democratic institutions while holding elections that retained a façade of legitimacy. In each case, the process was gradual and legalistic, making opposition appear premature or alarmist, until it was too late to reverse course.

Levitsky and Ziblatt emphasize that the true guardians of democracy are not only courts and constitutions, but norms: the unwritten rules of restraint, respect, and mutual toleration. When these norms are eroded, when political opponents become enemies, when winning becomes everything, when lies go unchallenged, the ground beneath democracy shifts.

This is the great danger of modern authoritarianism: it dresses itself in democratic clothing. It wins elections, speaks the language of the people, and claims to restore order. But behind the slogans is a deliberate strategy to demobilize dissent, concentrate power, and hollow out accountability. These regimes rarely announce their intentions; instead, they exploit the mechanisms of democracy, elections, legislatures, executive orders, not to serve the public, but to entrench power. The result is a system that retains its outer form while losing its democratic substance, creating a façade of legitimacy even as freedom erodes from within.

The antidote is not panic, but vigilance. Recognizing the signs, such as contempt for the press, delegitimization of opponents, threats to independent institutions, and erosion of electoral integrity, is the first step. These warning signs are not always dramatic; they often come cloaked in the language of reform or national pride. But the patterns are clear to those who are willing to look. The second step is civic renewal: a reinvestment in democratic education, discourse, and participation. This means not only voting, but defending institutions, teaching civic values, and practicing tolerance and dissent as democratic virtues. For once a democracy begins to die, its resurrection is far more difficult than its preservation, because what is lost is not just structure, but civic spirit, trust, and memory.

III. The Necessity of Resistance

Angela Davis reminds us in *Freedom Is a Constant Struggle* that democracy is not self-sustaining. It must be fought for—again and again, in every generation.

> "Freedom is a constant struggle. It requires persistent vigilance and active participation." — Angela Y. Davis, *Freedom Is a Constant Struggle*, 2016

Her global lens ties civil rights movements across the world together, making the case that protest, organization, and public education are indispensable acts of democratic defense. Davis draws parallels between struggles in Ferguson and Gaza, South Africa and Alabama, reminding us that oppression is global, and so is resistance.

Resistance, she argues, is not a singular act, but a culture. It requires habits of solidarity, critical consciousness, and institutional imagination. These movements did not emerge from chaos. They were built on political education, collective memory, and shared moral language. Civic literacy was their catalyst as much as civic courage. It is not enough to oppose injustice when it is convenient. A free society requires daily acts of engagement, from the protest line to the classroom, from the ballot box to the neighborhood meeting.

Frederick Douglass made a similar claim in his Fourth of July address. His message to America was both a condemnation and a challenge:

> "The limits of tyrants are prescribed by the endurance of those whom they oppress."

Douglass understood that silence enables oppression. Public indifference gives authoritarians free rein. His address was more than rhetoric; it was a demand for civic courage. The endurance of tyranny, he warned, is directly proportional to the complacency of the governed.

These insights are echoed in the histories of the U.S. Civil Rights Movement, South Africa's anti-apartheid struggle, and Poland's Solidarity movement. Each emerged from populations long denied power, and each demonstrated how organized resistance can bend history toward justice. From the Montgomery Bus Boycott to Soweto uprisings to the Gdańsk Shipyard strikes, these movements showed that democracy survives where people refuse to be silenced, and where they are prepared to suffer in order to speak.

Resistance also requires hope, not blind optimism, but strategic, grounded belief in the possibility of change. As history teaches, resistance rarely succeeds on the first attempt. But when pursued with resilience and vision, it becomes the seedbed of renewal. Democratic resilience is not born in the halls of power; it is forged in the streets, in the jails, in the libraries, and in the hearts of those who refuse to surrender to despair.

IV. The Role of the Intellectual and the Dissenter

Noam Chomsky, in *The Responsibility of Intellectuals*, argued that the educated have a duty to speak out; not as partisans, but as guardians of truth.

> "It is the responsibility of intellectuals to speak the truth and to expose lies." — Noam Chomsky, *The Responsibility of Intellectuals*, 1967

Christopher Hitchens carried that mantle in *Letters to a Young Contrarian*, framing dissent as not just a right but a moral obligation.

> "To be in opposition is not to be a nihilist. It's to be a free man." — Christopher Hitchens, *Letters to a Young Contrarian*, 2001

Together, they outline the ethical call to resist consensus when it veers toward repression. Education, in this light, is not about conformity. It is about the courage to stand alone. True education empowers the individual not to echo the crowd, but to challenge it when justice demands. It fosters the intellectual resilience needed to question dogma, critique authority, and endure isolation.

This principle has historical roots in figures like Václav Havel, the Czech dissident whose writing under communism laid the intellectual groundwork for democratic transition, and Andrei Sakharov, the Soviet physicist who used his status to challenge authoritarian lies. Their words helped galvanize underground resistance movements that ultimately reshaped national destinies.

In the United States, figures such as James Baldwin and Rachel Carson similarly wielded their intellect and moral clarity to challenge systemic injustice and catalyze public awareness. Baldwin confronted racial hypocrisy with unflinching honesty, while Carson defied corporate and governmental pressure to reveal the environmental cost of progress. In *Silent Spring*, she wrote, "We stand now where two roads diverge. But unlike the roads in Robert Frost's familiar poem, they are not equally fair. The road we have long been traveling is deceptively easy... but at its end lies disaster. The other fork of the road, the one less traveled by, offers our last, our only chance to reach a destination that assures the preservation of the earth." — Rachel Carson, *Silent Spring*, 1962 Their legacies affirm the power of the solitary voice raised in defense of reason and justice.

What unites these intellectuals is not their profession, but their purpose: to bear witness, to name what others avoid, and to insist on truth when lies are more convenient. In doing so, they exemplify the civic duty of dissent and remind us that democracies flourish only when their thinkers are unafraid to speak.

V. The Individual and the Loss of Civic Agency

Richard Wright's short story *The Man Who Was Almost a Man* is not a political tract, but it speaks volumes about maturity, power, and recognition. The protagonist, a young Black boy yearning to be seen as a man, buys a gun to assert his independence.

> "Ah swear fo' God! Ah'm goin' t' get a gun an' practice shootin'. Then Ah can be a man!" — Richard Wright, *The Man Who Was Almost a Man*, 1961

This moment of desperation reveals a deeper civic truth: in societies that deny people meaningful education, autonomy, and respect, rebellion becomes symbolic. Wright's story metaphorically critiques the systems that deny individuals the tools to participate as full citizens. The gun becomes not merely an object of power, but a surrogate for voice, legitimacy, and inclusion.

Wright's narrative resonates with broader historical patterns of exclusion. The environmental justice movement offers a compelling parallel. As Robert D. Bullard observed in *Dumping in*

Dixie, "Given the political climate of the dumps, and polluting industries... were likely to end up in somebody's backyard. But whose backyard? More often than not, these LULUs ended up in poor, powerless, black communities rather than in affluent suburbs." — Robert D. Bullard, *Dumping in Dixie: Race, Class, and Environmental Quality*, 1990 The same structural disregard that placed environmental hazards in marginalized communities also denied them avenues for protest and redress. For centuries, African Americans were systematically denied the franchise, access to quality education, and the protections of equal justice. The legacy of Jim Crow persists in modern forms, through voter suppression laws, gerrymandering, criminal disenfranchisement, and disparities in school funding. These policies do not just limit opportunity; they send a message that some citizens are less equal than others. Today, the denial of civic agency continues, not with overt exclusion, but with quiet policies that underfund schools, criminalize dissent, and redraw voting maps. A democracy that marginalizes its people trains them not to participate, but to withdraw.

Beyond race, similar dynamics affect marginalized groups across gender, class, and immigration status. Wherever people are denied access to education, silenced in public discourse, or pushed to the edges of power, democratic participation becomes performative rather than substantive. In these contexts, agency is not exercised. It is imagined, symbolized, or seized in protest.

Wright's story, though set in the early 20th century, remains a powerful allegory for how civic disempowerment breeds both personal frustration and systemic instability. A democracy that marginalizes its people creates the conditions for alienation, resistance, and ultimately, fracture. Full citizenship requires more than legal status. It demands dignity, opportunity, and a stake in the public square.

VI. Conclusion: History as a Warning, Resistance as a Duty

History does not merely offer dates and outcomes; it offers patterns and precedents. It reveals how political apathy allows opportunists to thrive, how lies erode public confidence, and how unchecked power silences voices until it is too late to resist. These are not the lessons of ancient history; they are the headlines of today.

The figures examined in this chapter show us that the fight for democracy requires more than outrage. It requires memory. It requires courage. It requires institutions fortified not just by laws, but by the moral convictions of the people who inhabit them. Above all, it requires citizens who understand that freedom is not inherited. It is earned and re-earned through constant engagement.

From the quiet acts of intellectual resistance to the mass movements that topple regimes, democratic renewal begins when ordinary people refuse to accept injustice as normal. It begins when they demand transparency, confront propaganda, resist mediocrity, and insist on full civic inclusion.

If democracy is to survive, it must be fought for—not just against the tyrant, but against the indifference that precedes him. Arendt, Douglass, Davis, Chomsky, and others issue the same warning: **truth must be defended, dissent must be practiced, and power must be questioned.**

This message echoes through the voices of cultural dissenters as well. Hunter S. Thompson warned, "Freedom is something that dies unless it's used," — quoted in *The Proud Highway: Saga of a Desperate Southern Gentleman*, 1997 — underscoring that liberty, left idle, decays into irrelevance. Jack Kerouac, with characteristic bluntness, offered a similar truth: "Better to sleep in an uncomfortable bed free, than sleep in a comfortable bed unfree."

— Jack Kerouac, *On the Road*, 1957. And Allen Ginsberg, in his howl of generational despair, exposed what happens when society loses its intellectual and moral bearings: "I saw the best minds of my generation destroyed by madness..." — Allen Ginsberg, *Howl*, 1956.

These voices, though unconventional, sharpen the same point made by the political theorists and activists discussed throughout this chapter: when truth is surrendered, resistance muted, and power left unchecked, democracy falters. Whether in the streets, the courts, or the pages of literature, the warning is clear. Freedom demands use, vigilance, and voice.

Democracy is not destroyed overnight. It erodes when citizens cease to care and it is preserved only when they choose to act. Cultural dissenters like Ginsberg, Thompson, and Kerouac captured the emotional undercurrent of this decay. Ginsberg mourned a generation lost to madness and silence. Thompson warned that unused freedom dies. Kerouac reminded us that even uncomfortable liberty is preferable to comfortable submission. Their insights underscore the urgency expressed by thinkers like Arendt, Douglass, Davis, and Chomsky, that democracy is not only threatened by tyrants, but by the widespread indifference and apathy that often precedes them. These voices, traditional and unconventional alike, converge on a common truth: truth must be defended, dissent must be practiced, and power must be questioned. These insights reinforce the political truths laid bare throughout this chapter: that when citizens disengage, institutions weaken, and when institutions weaken, democracy itself is imperiled.

The next chapter explores how democracy continues to weaken when public knowledge is undermined—when media becomes distorted, education is neglected, and civic memory is deliberately erased. If resistance begins with recognition, then the battle for democracy begins with reclaiming the institutions that shape how we know, remember, and think.

CHAPTER FOUR

*The Modern Mirror — Media,
Memory, and Misinformation*

*"What George Orwell feared were those who would ban books.
What Aldous Huxley feared was that there would be no reason to
ban a book, for there would be no one who wanted to read one."*
— Neil Postman, Amusing Ourselves to Death, 1985

In the twenty-first century, the threat to democracy is not
only political. It is cognitive. The machinery of modern
media, the architecture of digital platforms, and the erosion
of public education have converged to produce a society that
is increasingly disengaged from critical thought. Where the
ancient republics feared military coups and civil unrest, our crisis
arrives through entertainment, distraction, and manipulated
information flows. The civic foundation of democratic life,
public reasoning, factual literacy, and historical memory, is being
steadily undermined by systems that prioritize sensation over
substance.

Today, the dominant forces shaping political consciousness are
no longer classrooms or town halls, but curated timelines,

algorithmic feeds, and outrage-based programming. Citizens are rewarded not for questioning, but for conforming; not for examining facts, but for repeating narratives. The result is a population that may feel informed but is fundamentally disoriented; one that confuses repetition for truth and engagement for entertainment.

This chapter examines the modern forces that fracture democratic awareness and explores the consequences of a society that forgets how to think.

I. Postman's Warning: A Society Entertained to Death

In *Amusing Ourselves to Death*, Neil Postman contrasts the nightmares of Orwell and Huxley. Orwell feared oppression by force; Huxley feared oppression by pleasure. Postman concluded that the latter is the greater modern threat.

> "What George Orwell feared were those who would ban books. What Aldous Huxley feared was that there would be no reason to ban a book, for there would be no one who wanted to read one."

He argued that television, and by extension today's internet and social media, reduces public discourse to spectacle. When politics is indistinguishable from entertainment, truth is replaced by image, and democracy becomes performance. Public figures are no longer evaluated by their ideas or ethics, but by their ratings, optics, and ability to provoke emotion.

Postman warned that this transformation creates a shallow culture where civic reasoning is supplanted by slogan, and where complexity is drowned in noise. In such a society, the medium itself shapes the content: a soundbite-driven political system rewards charisma over coherence, and emotional resonance over factual rigor. Debate becomes performance. The citizen becomes a passive consumer.

This analysis proved prophetic during the 24-hour cable news boom and the rise of infotainment in American politics. Shows that blend news with comedy or outrage blur lines between information and manipulation. In Italy, media tycoon Silvio Berlusconi used television ownership to dominate political messaging and sideline serious debate, demonstrating how entertainment monopolies can control democratic discourse. More recently, social media platforms have amplified these trends, rewarding viral content over verified truth and further eroding the distinction between fact, opinion, and fiction.

Postman's core message remains urgent: a democracy cannot survive if its citizens lose the capacity, or the desire, to think beyond the immediate, the entertaining, or the superficial.

II. The Bludgeon of Propaganda

Noam Chomsky, revisiting the dynamics of media and democracy, emphasized the systemic nature of misinformation in free societies. In democratic contexts, coercion is often unnecessary because people are shaped by subtle yet pervasive channels of propaganda.

> "Propaganda is to a democracy what the bludgeon is to a totalitarian state." — Noam Chomsky, *Media Control: The Spectacular Achievements of Propaganda*, 1997

Modern citizens are not silenced. hey are inundated. Truth becomes diluted amid a flood of opinions, distractions, and carefully curated falsehoods. In such an environment, education must equip citizens not just with knowledge, but with the tools to *discern* truth from manipulation.

Chomsky's analysis draws attention to the fact that democratic societies are uniquely vulnerable to non-coercive forms of narrative control, precisely because their freedoms allow for a diversity of voices, many of which are commodified, co-opted, or drowned out. Rather than suppress dissent through violence, modern propaganda works by creating an environment of confusion and contradiction, where truth competes with a thousand half-truths.

This warning is evident in Russia's hybrid model of state-controlled and pseudo-independent media, where narratives are manufactured to foster cynicism rather than loyalty. Similarly, during the Iraq War, the strategic messaging of weapons of mass destruction exemplified how democratic governments can deploy narrative control to bypass public skepticism when media is complicit or passive.

Even in Western democracies, corporate media consolidation, partisan echo chambers, and the rise of influencer-driven commentary have blurred the line between journalism and entertainment, further distorting the public's grasp of fact and fiction. In such a climate, the citizen's role is not merely to consume information, but to interrogate it; an ability that must be taught, cultivated, and protected if democracy is to endure.

III. Mill Revisited: The Death of Originality

John Stuart Mill warned of another kind of tyranny—the tyranny of conformism. In *On Liberty*, he wrote:

> "Originality is the one thing which unoriginal minds cannot feel the use of." — John Stuart Mill, *On Liberty*, 1859

In an age of algorithms and curated feeds, Mill's warning takes on new urgency. When everyone is fed what they already believe, dissent becomes deviant. The homogeneity of opinion becomes not just a social norm, but a market preference. Democracy withers when its citizens cease to challenge, question, or imagine alternatives.

Mill believed that the vitality of a free society depends on its willingness to tolerate eccentricity, experimentation, and the clash of ideas. Original thinkers, those willing to voice unpopular truths, are essential not because they are always right, but because they challenge the intellectual status quo. In a healthy democracy, the individual who thinks differently is not a threat to social order, but a necessary engine of progress.

Historically, this fear was realized in the McCarthy era, when ideological conformity was enforced by a culture of fear and public shaming. Careers and reputations were destroyed for mere association with dissenting political views. Today, cancel culture on both the left and the right can serve a similar function, policing speech not through law, but through social and economic coercion.

Moreover, educational and professional environments that reward consensus over curiosity create citizens who are trained to fit in rather than think critically. A society that suppresses originality, whether through peer pressure, censorship, or algorithmic invisibility, creates a population less capable of addressing complex problems or resisting groupthink.

Mill's defense of liberty is ultimately a defense of mental freedom. Without it, public discourse becomes stagnant, policy becomes reactive, and democracy becomes brittle, unable to adapt to new challenges or include new voices.

IV. Education or Indoctrination?

Public education was once conceived as the engine of democratic citizenship. Today, it is a battlefield, over history, identity, curriculum, and truth itself. The erosion of civic education has left students unprepared for critical analysis, historical understanding, or democratic participation. Instead of learning how to think, many are taught what to think, or worse, taught nothing at all.

The result? Generations who do not recognize democratic

backsliding because they have never seen democracy properly taught or practiced. When schools prioritize test scores over inquiry, compliance over curiosity, and memorization over discussion, they produce citizens who may be trained, but not truly educated. This deficiency does not manifest only in ignorance, but in civic fragility: a population unprepared to recognize demagoguery, defend pluralism, or engage in reasoned dissent.

Historical parallels can be drawn with the Third Reich's use of textbooks and youth education to inculcate loyalty to Nazi ideology. In the American South, Lost Cause mythology dominated curricula for decades, perpetuating falsehoods about slavery and the Civil War. Today, debates over how race, gender, and history are taught in U.S. schools echo these struggles. Wherever education becomes a tool of ideological conformity rather than intellectual empowerment, democracy is at risk.

This tension is also visible in modern efforts to politicize school boards, restrict library content, and censor discussions about social justice. The result is an education system increasingly shaped by fear rather than freedom, where students learn to repeat rather than reason. A functioning democracy cannot tolerate this trend. As Thomas Jefferson wrote, "If a nation expects to be ignorant and free, in a state of civilization, it expects what never was and never will be." — Thomas Jefferson, Letter to Colonel Charles Yancey, January 6, 1816

Isaac Asimov echoed this concern in a now-famous critique of anti-intellectualism in democratic culture: "There is a cult of ignorance in the United States, and there has always been. The strain of anti-intellectualism has been a constant thread winding its way through our political and cultural life, nurtured by the false notion that democracy means that 'my ignorance is just as good as your knowledge.'" Asimov warned that scientific and civic illiteracy would become fatal weaknesses in a democratic society that values opinion over understanding.

Isaac Asimov's now-famous quote was not merely a critique of educational gaps. It was a prophetic diagnosis of a growing cultural illness: the celebration of opinion unmoored from evidence, and the suspicion that intellectuals are enemies of the people.

This anti-intellectual strain, once confined to the margins, has become a recurring feature of populist movements across the globe. In such movements, expertise is often cast as elitism, and the academy is portrayed as a bastion of corruption or indoctrination. Scientists, journalists, and educators are framed not as stewards of public knowledge, but as conspirators against "real people." Public discourse becomes defined not by facts, but by feelings—by the raw force of assertion rather than the careful work of analysis.

Populism in this form thrives not on dialogue, but on division. It frames complexity as a trick, nuance as betrayal, and disagreement as disloyalty. The result is a civic culture in which education itself is treated with suspicion, and in which those who ask hard questions are viewed as enemies of the truth. At its most dangerous, anti-intellectual populism becomes a tool for authoritarian leaders to delegitimize dissent, control narratives, and hollow out institutions of learning and accountability.

We have seen this play out across history: during the Cultural Revolution in China, when teachers and scholars were targeted for "bourgeois thinking"; in Nazi Germany, where entire disciplines were purged for their refusal to conform; and more recently, in the deliberate dismantling of curriculum standards in democratic states to suppress critical discussions of race, gender, and history.

In the United States, the attacks on public universities, science funding, and school curricula are not isolated incidents; they are symptoms of a deeper civic crisis: a rejection of the very idea that truth must be pursued, tested, and taught. When public leaders assert that "I alone can fix it," or that "nobody knows the system better than me," they are not just displaying hubris. They are modeling contempt for collaborative knowledge and democratic deliberation.

Asimov feared that a democratic society that devalues knowledge would not long remain a democracy. His warning remains urgent today. For when facts are optional, and reasoning is a liability, democracy becomes a hollow ritual. Its foundation eaten away by the very ignorance it was meant to overcome.

V. Conclusion: Reclaiming the Mind

This chapter's authors remind us that **a republic cannot endure if its people forget how to think**. The threats we face today are not tanks in the streets but pixels on a screen, not banned books but unread ones, not iron-fisted dictators but soft distractions that erode reason.

To protect democracy, we must first protect the mind. That means restoring critical thinking, defending public education, and demanding a media culture that informs rather than entertains. Without these foundations, freedom becomes an illusion and the republic becomes a memory.

The erosion of intellectual engagement does not happen all at once. It begins with the sidelining of humanities education, the politicization of school boards, and the treatment of dissenting voices as dangerous rather than necessary. It accelerates when media systems reward attention over accuracy, and when fact becomes just one opinion among many. Left unaddressed, it culminates in a citizenry incapable of deliberation, vulnerable to manipulation, and indifferent to its own disempowerment.

Democracy is not simply a structure of government, it is a habit of mind. It requires that individuals take seriously their role as participants in public life: questioning, listening, challenging, and learning. A republic survives not through ritual but through reasoning. And it thrives when its people refuse to trade thought for comfort, knowledge for noise, or agency for ease.

To reclaim the republic, we must first reclaim the mind; not in isolation, but in community. That reclamation begins in classrooms, libraries, living rooms, and town halls. It begins with the courage to think out loud and the humility to listen well. It begins, most of all, with remembering that freedom is not self-renewing. It is a discipline we must choose, every day.

The next chapter turns to the constitutional and civic foundations that must hold firm if the republic is to survive, trust, pluralism, public institutions, and the living Constitution itself. Before we examine the people who defend democracy, we must first understand the structures they are trying to preserve.

Libraries, public, free, and pluralistic, are among the last truly democratic institutions, offering sanctuary for truth-seeking in an age of distraction. It examines the federal employees, attorneys, educators, and activists who serve as the human guardrails of democracy, defending its principles not from ideology, but from erosion.

CHAPTER FIVE

Foundations Worth Defending
— Trust, Virtue, and the
American Framework

"The Constitution is not a suicide pact." — Justice Robert H.
Jackson, Terminiello v. City of Chicago, 337 U.S. 1 (1949),
dissenting opinion

D emocracy, like a building, does not rest on sentiment. It rests on structure. And though the American system was designed with tension and imperfection, its architecture is more than functional: it is flexible, resilient, and worthy of defense. Yet that defense requires understanding. In this chapter, we turn to the constitutional foundations and cultural commitments that make democratic self-government possible. We also confront the fragility of those foundations, from declining public trust to the vanishing of local journalism. This is not a chapter of nostalgia. It is a sober reckoning with what is required to preserve the system we have, and how to improve it from within.

I. Trust: The Hidden Infrastructure of Democracy

At the core of any democratic society is trust, not blind faith, but a working confidence in systems, processes, and fellow citizens. We trust that votes will be counted honestly, that courts will interpret laws fairly, and that the peaceful transfer of power will be respected. When trust erodes, participation withers. Cynicism replaces engagement. And democracy dies by attrition, not assault.

Restoring democratic trust begins at the community level. Citizens are more likely to trust what they can see: local courts, school boards, and election offices. Transparency, responsiveness, and accountability are not luxuries, they are democratic necessities. Transparency, in particular, is the foundation upon which trust and legitimacy are built. It means more than just public access to information. It requires that information be timely, accessible, and understandable. Whether through budget disclosures, voting records, agency reports, or public forums, transparency turns opaque power into visible responsibility. When government operates behind closed doors, suspicion takes root. But when it engages in open dialogue and shared governance, citizens are more likely to believe not only in what government does, but in why it does it.

Trust is rebuilt through clear, consistent, and participatory governance. For example, participatory budgeting initiatives in cities like New York and Chicago have shown how involving citizens directly in financial decisions increases both transparency and trust. Similarly, the expansion of community policing programs, where officers build relationships within the neighborhoods they serve, has led to more effective public safety and improved public confidence in law enforcement.

Rebuilding trust also involves public accountability. When school boards, city councils, or election offices openly share their deliberations, livestream meetings, respond to public inquiries, and publish accessible financial data, they signal respect for the citizen. That visibility fosters legitimacy. And when mistakes are made, acknowledging them forthrightly, rather than deflecting blame, becomes an act of democratic repair. Ultimately, trust is not a gift citizens give their government. It is something governments must earn, daily, through ethical behavior and inclusive process.

II. Journalism: The Local Press as a Civic Lifeline

While national media grabs attention, it is local journalism that exposes corruption, informs the electorate, and builds civic identity. The disappearance of local newspapers, over 2,500 in the past two decades, has created news deserts where public accountability disappears with them. When no one covers city council meetings or audits school district budgets, misinformation fills the void.

Supporting local media, through subscriptions, public funding models, and media literacy, is as crucial as defending voting rights. The press, especially at the community level, is not the enemy of the people. It is one of democracy's last defenses.

By contrast, social media is not journalism. While it can amplify news and connect communities, it lacks the editorial oversight, ethical standards, and verification mechanisms that define professional reporting. Algorithms on major platforms are engineered for engagement, not truth, often pushing sensational content into echo chambers that reinforce biases rather than challenge them.

Social media can be easily manipulated, by bots, propaganda campaigns, and coordinated disinformation efforts. The result is a civic environment polluted with outrage and distortion. Without the counterbalance of trusted local journalism and an informed public, social media can corrode the very deliberative processes democracy requires. Civic literacy in the digital age must include the ability to distinguish between credible reporting and algorithmic noise.

III. Civic Virtue: The Moral Center of Republican Governance

The Founders did not assume virtue. They demanded it. Civic virtue, placing public good above personal gain, is the animating spirit of the republic. It is not perfection. It is the disciplined choice to act on principle when convenience tempts otherwise. It is George Washington stepping down from power. It is whistleblowers exposing misconduct. It is everyday citizens showing up to serve without fanfare.

Virtue, unlike law, cannot be mandated. It must be cultivated, through education, community, and moral example. Civic virtue gives a republic its moral coherence, grounding the rights of the individual in the responsibilities of the citizen. It is what compels someone to vote even when it's inconvenient, to serve on a jury with integrity, or to defend the rights of others even when they disagree.

When civic virtue declines, cynicism and self-interest fill the vacuum. Public service becomes performative, institutions lose credibility, and corruption gains ground. This is why virtue must be modeled in families, reinforced in schools, honored in public discourse, and demanded of leaders. Without it, the mechanics of democracy may continue to grind, but the soul of the republic erodes. A republic without virtue is not only unstable. It is unsustainable.

IV. Pluralism: Strength in Difference

American democracy is not homogenous by design. It is pluralistic. A system premised on the coexistence of varied beliefs, traditions, and viewpoints. Pluralism is not relativism. It does not demand we agree on everything, but that we commit to live with our disagreements peacefully, under shared rules and mutual respect.

In an age of ideological silos, pluralism is both more difficult and more necessary. It requires listening beyond one's tribe. It requires shared facts and agreed-upon processes. It requires that we remember that our opponents in politics are not our enemies in democracy.

This commitment to pluralism is not theoretical, it is operational. It informs how we build coalitions, how we shape public discourse, and how we navigate disagreement without descending into dysfunction. As will be discussed in the concluding chapter on civic action, the habit of democracy is built not just by voting or protesting, but by engaging those with whom we disagree. Supporting inclusive civic institutions, defending the right of others to speak, even when we oppose their views, and building relationships across lines of ideology or identity are all ways in which pluralism becomes a living practice. Without it, the Constitution's promise of liberty for all collapses into liberty for the loudest.

Preserving a pluralistic republic means elevating dialogue over division, courage over comfort, and patience over polarization. It is the daily work of recognizing humanity before ideology and choosing participation over purity.

V. Pluralism in Practice: Responding Together in Crisis

Pluralism is not just a theory, it is tested in moments of crisis, when competing beliefs and identities must still find common ground. One striking example emerged after the 9/11 attacks, when religious pluralism faced an immediate threat. As anti-Muslim sentiment surged, interfaith organizations like the Interfaith Youth Core, Shoulder to Shoulder, and local coalitions across cities like Chicago, Los Angeles, and New York mobilized to affirm religious freedom, combat scapegoating, and protect community members from violence.

These weren't abstract gestures. In many neighborhoods, rabbis stood beside imams. Catholic priests marched with Muslim civic leaders. Sikh community centers opened their doors to non-Sikhs for teach-ins and public dialogue. In Boston, a coalition of Jewish, Muslim, and Christian leaders released a joint statement rejecting religious bigotry and reminding the public that "an attack on one faith is an attack on all."

Pluralism proved not just morally necessary, but operationally effective. It reduced violence, restored social cohesion, and reminded citizens that democratic strength lies in difference respected, not erased. In moments of upheaval, it was shared citizenship, not shared creed, that sustained the public square.

VI. The Administrative Procedure Act: Democracy in Slow Motion

A lesser-known but critical safeguard of democracy is the Administrative Procedure Act (APA) of 1946. Often described as the "bill of rights for the administrative state," the APA ensures that federal agencies, many of which write and enforce binding rules, do so transparently, predictably, and with public input.

The APA requires agencies to publish proposed rules, provide opportunities for public comment, and offer reasoned explanations for final decisions. It prohibits arbitrary action, protects due process, and allows courts to review agency decisions. In short, it codifies the idea that power must be both technically competent and publicly accountable.

The APA may not stir public emotion, but it is among the quiet guardrails that prevent democratic slippage. When enforced properly, it ensures that regulations are not written in secret, that special interests must justify their requests, and that agencies remain tethered to the people they serve.

Citizens, journalists, attorneys, and advocates can all engage in this process, not just by challenging bad rules after the fact, but by submitting comments, testifying, or demanding transparency during rulemaking. Participation here is a powerful form of vigilance.

VII. Oversight and Transparency: Holding Power to Account

In a constitutional republic, Congress is not just a lawmaking body, it is a watchdog. The Founders gave it oversight powers so that no branch, including the executive, could operate with impunity. This oversight is not optional. It is a fundamental duty of representation.

Yet in recent years, congressional oversight has faltered. Hearings have become spectacles. Investigations are too often partisan theater rather than tools for truth-seeking. What was designed to ensure accountability has, in many cases, become another front in the culture war.

This is where citizen vigilance matters most.

Citizens must demand that their representatives engage in real oversight, not performative outrage. They must pressure lawmakers to fund Inspectors General (OIGs), protect whistleblowers, and respect the constitutional duty of inquiry. Oversight is only as effective as the public pressure behind it.

One of the most accessible oversight tools available to the public is the Freedom of Information Act (FOIA). Passed in 1966, FOIA gives citizens the right to request documents from federal agencies, a radical shift that made secrecy the exception, not the rule. Journalists use it to uncover corruption. Activists use it to track enforcement gaps. Ordinary citizens use it to understand what government is doing in their name.

But FOIA only works if people use it. If they challenge unjust denials. If they hold agencies accountable for delays. If they follow up and share what they learn. The same applies to the Office of the Inspector General system, a network of internal watchdogs across agencies. OIG reports, when read and shared, become tools of civic oversight. They flag waste, fraud, abuse, and ethical failures long before the headlines appear, if anyone is paying attention.

If democracy is to be preserved, citizens must not only vote. They must watch. They must ask. They must show elected officials that passive representation is not enough. Congressional oversight, FOIA, and the OIGs are instruments of public accountability, but only if the public demands their use.

VIII. The Constitution: A Living Framework

The U.S. Constitution is not just parchment and precedent. It is a living framework, designed to endure by adapting. While its original structure was revolutionary, its longevity comes from its capacity for amendment, reinterpretation, and engagement. Citizens shape the Constitution not only through courts and Congress, but through protest, education, and advocacy.

Rigid originalism denies this dynamic truth. Just as a healthy society must evolve, so must its legal frameworks. The Constitution is not sacred because it is unchanging. It is sacred because it creates the conditions for a society that can govern itself, if its people are willing to participate.

The Constitution was designed to be amended, interpreted, and enforced, not by elites alone, but by the people through their elected representatives and institutions. The formal process of amendment, outlined in Article V, is deliberately difficult to ensure seriousness and consensus. But the Constitution is also changed through interpretation, by the courts responding to new realities, and by legislatures crafting laws that respond to the Constitution's open-ended clauses.

Equally important is enforcement. The Constitution has no army. Its strength lies in the will of citizens to demand its protections and insist on its promises. Every generation is called to interpret what liberty, equality, and justice mean in their own time, and to compel their representatives to act accordingly. That work is not optional. It is the core function of citizenship in a democratic republic.

IX. Conclusion: Strengthened by Understanding

To borrow Lincoln's warning: a house divided cannot stand, but a house misunderstood cannot be defended. If we do not understand the foundations of our system, trust, virtue, pluralism, and constitutional adaptability, we will not recognize when they begin to fail. Nor will we know how to repair them.

The task ahead is not just to guard democracy, but to understand what we are guarding. The republic is resilient. But it is not self-sustaining.

It depends, still, on us.

CHAPTER SIX

Stewards of the Republic

"The success of a government, especially a democratic one, depends more on the character of its citizens than on any written constitution." — Louis Brandeis, Whitney v. California, 274 U.S. 357 (1927), concurring opinion

Democracy is often discussed as a structure of laws, institutions, and electoral processes. But these are only the visible scaffolds. The true support beams, the unseen guardrails, are the individuals who choose to uphold democratic norms in their daily work, in their communities, and in moments of public crisis. They are federal employees who refuse to carry out unlawful orders. Attorneys who defend constitutional principles above client interests. Activists who speak when silence is safer. And ordinary citizens who resist the pull of apathy.

"...the charge that I tell anyone is that a democracy is only as strong as the people that participate in it. And I don't care if you are not old enough to vote, or you're one of our elders, we need you to participate in that democracy. And you do so by speaking up. It's your first amendment right to be vocal; to also ask for address from your government as a fundamental right that the founding fathers understood was what is needed if you're going to have a thriving Republic with Democratic values, and so I ask each and every American to make sure that your voice is heard, and you can do that in a number of ways." — Charles F. "Chuck" Sams III, remarks at "Consider This: The Lands We Live On with Chuck Sams," Town Hall Presentation, Oregon Humanities, Pendleton Center for the Arts, Pendleton, OR, April 9, 2025.

In a time when faith in institutions is eroding, it is these people who remind us that democracy is not automated. It is not sustained by default. It requires attention, resistance, and renewal.

This chapter turns to the human infrastructure of democracy: the people whose ethical commitments, professional duties, and civic courage form the last line of defense when systems falter. They are not always celebrated. Often, they are marginalized, punished, or ignored. But without them, democratic self-government becomes hollow.

From federal whistleblowers to community organizers, public interest lawyers to principled bureaucrats, these individuals exemplify what Hannah Arendt called the capacity for action, the power of one person to say, "no," when it matters most. Their stories remind us that democratic collapse is not inevitable, and neither is democratic survival. What matters is whether enough people are willing to stand between the public and its undoing.

This chapter is a tribute to those people. It argues that in an age of institutional fragility and rising authoritarianism, **the republic is ultimately guarded by conscience, not just constitutions**.

I. The Federal Workforce: Silent Stewards of the Republic

"Endeavors succeed or fail because of the people involved. Only by attracting the best people will you accomplish great deeds." — Colin Powell, *My American Journey* (1995)

This insight from General Colin Powell underscores the critical role that dedicated, principled federal workers play in sustaining the machinery of democracy. The daily operations of government, the continuity of services, and the ethical enforcement of laws all depend on the character and commitment of these individuals.

Behind every law passed by Congress... and every regulation debated in the press, there is a cadre of career civil servants quietly doing the work of governance. These individuals, scientists, analysts, inspectors, clerks, park rangers, auditors, foreign service officers, form the administrative backbone of democratic life.

They are tasked not only with executing public policy but with preserving institutional memory, protecting procedural fairness, and upholding the rule of law through daily decisions that rarely make headlines. In polarized times, they are often dismissed as part of a faceless "deep state" or derided for bureaucratic inertia. But history shows that when democracy is under pressure, it is often these very individuals who refuse to bend.

During the Watergate crisis, federal employees in the Department of Justice and the FBI helped expose and resist the abuses of executive power. Inspectors General across multiple agencies have uncovered fraud, waste, and political interference, often at personal and professional cost. The peaceful functioning of elections, the protection of environmental and public health standards, the integrity of scientific research within government, all depend on the quiet diligence of these public servants.

During the Trump administration, multiple career officials publicly challenged political manipulation of scientific reports, intelligence briefings, and foreign policy. In the 2020 election cycle, state and local election workers upheld the security and legitimacy of vote counting despite enormous pressure and threats of violence.

Reflecting on his early experiences as a sailor visiting national parks and monuments, Charles F. "Chuck" Sams III emphasized how witnessing America's diverse histories reinforced his military oath to protect the Constitution. He noted that National Park Service staff share this same oath, acting as dedicated stewards who safeguard not only the parks themselves but also the foundational democratic ideals they represent, by faithfully preserving and telling the full story of America's diverse heritage.—Charles F. "Chuck" Sams III, remarks at "Consider This: The Lands We Live On with Chuck Sams," Town Hall Presentation, Oregon Humanities, Pendleton Center for the Arts, Pendleton, OR, April 9, 2025.

These federal and state workers exemplify what it means to serve not a party, but a people. Their oath is not to a leader, but to the Constitution. They are not elected, but they are accountable; to the law, to ethical norms, and to the enduring principles of impartial public service.

Their work may go unnoticed. Their names may be unknown. But in every democracy that survives moments of stress, there are stewards like these holding the line between partisanship and principle.

Horace Albright, one of the early directors of the National Park Service, once said: "If a trail is to be blazed, it is 'send a ranger.' If an animal is floundering in the snow, a ranger is sent to pull him out; if a bear is in the hotel, if a fire threatens a forest, if someone is to be saved, it is 'send a ranger.'" This quote underscores the remarkable breadth and quiet heroism of public servants. Albright's reflection, though rooted in the context of national parks, captures the essence of federal service across all domains. People called to act, often without recognition, to preserve the integrity and safety of the public trust. Their loyalty is not to outcomes, but to process. And in that loyalty, they protect the very idea of the republic.

II. Lawyers and Legal Professionals: Guardians of the Constitutional Order

Lawyers occupy a unique space in a democracy. They are interpreters of the law, advocates for the vulnerable, and, at their best, guardians of the constitutional framework. The legal profession is not merely a career path; it is a civic role grounded in ethical obligation.

Throughout American history, attorneys have stood at the intersection of power and accountability. In landmark civil rights cases like *Brown v. Board of Education*, they dismantled the legal foundations of segregation. In the Pentagon Papers case, legal advocates defended the right of the press to inform the public about government deception. In immigration courts, public defenders continue to stand between vulnerable individuals and the unchecked power of the state.

Attorneys also play a critical role in resisting overreach from within the legal system itself. Government lawyers, judges, and legal scholars have refused to validate unconstitutional orders and have spoken out against partisan interference in judicial processes. Their principled dissent upholds the core tenet that the law serves the people, not those who temporarily wield power.

The rule of law depends not just on statutes, but on the daily practice of lawyers who are willing to say, "this is unlawful," even when doing so comes with personal cost. Legal ethics, professional standards, and constitutional interpretation are not abstract. They are lived out in the courtroom, in agency proceedings, and in legal scholarship that frames national debate.

In times of crisis, lawyers can serve as instruments of suppression or liberation. The difference lies in whether they see themselves as servants of power, or as stewards of principle. In a democratic republic, the legal profession is one of the final guardrails. When it fails, the system bends more easily toward tyranny. When it stands firm, even in silence, it reminds us that democracy has defenders not only in the streets, but also in the courts.

III. Activists and Concerned Citizens: Democracy's Nervous System

"Where you see wrong or inequality or injustice, speak out, because this is your country. This is your democracy. Make it. Protect it. Pass it on." — Thurgood Marshall, speech at Howard University (1978)

While institutions provide structure, it is movements that often provide momentum. Activists and engaged citizens form the nervous system of democracy; alert to injustice, responsive to emerging threats, and often the first to mobilize when official channels fail.

From the abolitionists and suffragists of the 19th century to the civil rights organizers, anti-war protesters, and environmental advocates of the 20th, these individuals and movements have forced the nation to confront its failures and extend its promises. They remind us that the Constitution is not self-executing. It requires pressure from below to fulfill its moral and legal commitments.

Today's movements, whether focused on racial justice, climate change, voting rights, LGBTQ+ equality, or economic fairness, continue this legacy. They use protest, litigation, lobbying, and storytelling to engage the public and pressure the state. Their work not only pushes policy but reshapes public consciousness.

In repressive environments, activism is often criminalized. Yet history vindicates those who risked safety and reputation to challenge unjust laws and expose abuses. From John Lewis crossing the Edmund Pettus Bridge to Greta Thunberg standing before world leaders, these acts of courage resonate because they are rooted in principle and aimed at awakening democratic accountability.

Concerned citizens may never organize a march or file a lawsuit. But they contribute in important ways, voting consistently, serving on school boards, attending town halls, challenging disinformation, and teaching democratic values to the next generation. Their collective efforts form the cultural infrastructure of freedom.

Democracy does not live in marble buildings or parchment texts. It lives in people; in their voices, choices, and unrelenting belief that the system can work better because it must. When citizens act, they reanimate the democratic experiment and remind institutions who they were built to serve.

IV. When Conscience Confronts Power: The Whistleblower's Role

Perhaps no figure more clearly embodies the tension between individual ethics and institutional power than the whistleblower. These are the people who, when faced with wrongdoing, choose to speak up, often at extraordinary personal risk. They do not act out of partisanship or opportunism, but from a belief that the truth matters more than their comfort, career, or safety.

Whistleblowers operate across all sectors, government, military, journalism, technology, and their actions have often been essential in defending democratic accountability. Daniel Ellsberg's release of the Pentagon Papers exposed government deception about the Vietnam War. Edward Snowden's disclosures raised urgent questions about privacy, surveillance, and constitutional rights in the digital age. More recently, whistleblowers from the Centers for Disease Control, the National Security Council, and Facebook have challenged narratives that concealed public harm.

These individuals are not always celebrated. They are frequently attacked, fired, prosecuted, or silenced. Yet their sacrifices illuminate the moral fault lines in institutions where loyalty to authority is too often placed above loyalty to the public interest.

The legal protections for whistleblowers vary widely, and are often inadequate. But the ethical imperative they fulfill remains clear: in moments when the machinery of power is being misused, the courage of a single voice can bring accountability back into focus.

Democracies cannot afford to treat whistleblowers as anomalies. They are not rebels against the republic, but stewards of its integrity. By exposing hidden abuses, they allow the rest of society to correct course. Their warnings are not betrayals. They are acts of loyalty to a higher civic ideal.

> "The first requisite of a good citizen in this Republic of ours is that he shall be able and willing to pull his own weight; that he shall not be a mere passenger, but shall do his share in the work that each generation of us finds ready to hand; and, furthermore, that in doing his work he shall show, not only the capacity for sturdy self-help, but also self-respecting regard for the rights of others." — Theodore Roosevelt, speech in New York City (1903)

V. Toward a Culture of Constitutional Duty

What unites public servants, legal advocates, activists, and whistleblowers is not ideology but an ethic. A shared belief that the principles enshrined in the Constitution are not self-enforcing and that defending them requires personal action. These individuals practice what might be called *constitutional duty*: a civic orientation that puts loyalty to democratic norms above partisanship, careerism, or fear.

Constitutional duty is not abstract. It manifests in daily

decisions: a government employee refusing to manipulate data; a lawyer upholding legal rights for an unpopular client; a teacher empowering students to ask hard questions. It happens in boardrooms, classrooms, courthouses, and around kitchen tables. Less about ceremony than conscience.

Fostering this culture requires more than professional codes. It demands a reinvestment in civic education, institutional ethics, and public leadership that affirms the role of service, truth-telling, and dissent. It also requires that institutions reward, not punish, those who act in defense of democratic integrity.

We cannot rely solely on laws to protect the republic. Laws are tools; their just application depends on the people entrusted with enforcing them. The durability of a democracy depends on citizens who understand not only their rights but also their responsibilities, and who are prepared to act when those responsibilities are threatened.

In the end, constitutional duty is not about heroism. It is about habits, habits of truth, accountability, service, and sacrifice. These are not dramatic gestures, but the daily practices that reinforce democratic life. They are the quiet commitments that keep the republic alive. The habit of truth. The habit of accountability. The habit of putting country before comfort and principle before party. These are the everyday acts that sustain the republic.

VI. Conclusion: Citizenship as the Final Safeguard

We have now seen how individuals, not just institutions, form the final line of defense in a functioning democracy. In each chapter of this book, we have encountered warnings about what happens when citizens stop thinking, stop questioning, and stop participating. But we have also seen what it looks like when they do the opposite; when they challenge, protect, and preserve.

The people profiled in this chapter are not outliers. They are models of what it means to live in a republic, people who act not out of convenience or vanity, but out of obligation to the idea that freedom is a shared inheritance. They are living reminders that democracy is not preserved by sentiment alone. It is preserved by people who show up.

Every system, no matter how elegant, can fail. Every safeguard, no matter how robust, can be weakened. What keeps democracy alive is not the strength of its slogans or the grandeur of its ideals, but the quiet resolve of those who choose, every day, to stand between decay and renewal.

CHAPTER SEVEN

The Work of Citizenship
— A Call to Action

"The most important political office is that of the private citizen."
— Louis Brandeis, quoted in Whitney v. California, 1927

Democracy is not sustained by elections alone. It endures through the habits, choices, and courage of those who live within it. Having journeyed through the history, theory, fiction, and lived experience of democratic erosion and resistance, this final chapter turns from observation to obligation. It asks not only what threatens democracy, but what protects it. Not just who tears it down, but who builds it up.

The answer, as always, is us.

Citizenship is not merely a status. It is a practice. And like any practice, it must be cultivated intentionally, through daily habits, shared commitments, and the willingness to act. This chapter outlines concrete ways that individuals can defend and strengthen the institutions, values, and civic culture that democracy requires.

In an age of distraction, polarization, and disinformation, many feel powerless. But democracy is not maintained by the powerful. It is preserved by the vigilant, those who understand that freedom depends not only on resisting tyranny but on sustaining the conditions that make liberty possible.

Alexis de Tocqueville observed in 1835 that "the health of a democratic society may be measured by the quality of functions performed by private citizens." — Alexis de Tocqueville, *Democracy in America*, 1835 That truth has not changed. The republic survives not on passive observation, but on active stewardship.

The following sections offer a framework for civic responsibility in the 21st century. They are neither exhaustive nor prescriptive, but they are urgent. Because if the chapters before have shown anything, it is that the republic cannot keep itself. That work belongs to all of us.

I. The Habits of a Vigilant Citizen

Before citizens can change their communities, they must cultivate the mindset and behaviors that sustain democracy from within. Personal responsibility is where public accountability begins.

Democracy is built on habits, small, daily choices that shape the political culture in which we live. The vigilant citizen does not wait for a crisis to care about their country. They stay engaged even when the stakes feel low, the outcomes uncertain, or the news discouraging. The habits listed below are neither glamorous nor headline-grabbing. But they are essential.

Read Widely and Critically

An engaged citizen is a well-informed one. That means reading across disciplines and perspectives, not just headlines, but history, law, philosophy, and literature. Reading sharpens judgment and builds the intellectual humility necessary to participate meaningfully in civic life. It also means digging into local sources, city budgets, legislation, school board decisions, so that participation is grounded in real understanding, not just opinion.

Verify, Don't Amplify

In an age of disinformation, reposting or reacting without fact-checking fuels the very confusion that weakens democracy. The vigilant citizen pauses before sharing, checks multiple credible sources, and seeks context before outrage. Understand the difference between evidence and speculation, and learn how to spot doctored images, misleading headlines, or manipulated data. A democracy drowning in misinformation cannot reason its way forward. Every share, comment, or repost is a civic act, and should be treated with the same seriousness as a vote.

Practice Civil Discourse

Democracy depends on disagreement, but disagreement must be principled. Listen to understand, not just to rebut. Challenge ideas without degrading people. The way we argue matters as much as the ideas we advance. Civil discourse is not the absence of passion. It is the presence of respect. It means making room for complexity, asking clarifying questions, and remembering that behind every opinion is a person. Democracy suffers when we turn opponents into enemies instead of treating them as fellow citizens with different views on a shared future.

Be Present, Not Just Opinionated

It's easy to comment. It's harder to show up. Vigilant citizens attend meetings, read public notices, and ask questions. They do the slow, often invisible work of civic presence that builds trust and holds local power accountable.

Democracy is not sustained by intensity alone. It is sustained by consistency. The habits of vigilance are not extraordinary. But practiced widely, they can make a republic resilient.

A Citizen's Story: Standing Up for the Bookshelf

In a small Midwestern town, a mother of two noticed something troubling at her local public library: a new policy quietly removed books about race, gender identity, and historical injustice from youth shelves after pressure from a vocal minority on the library board. The books weren't banned outright, but made functionally invisible.

Rather than rage on social media or retreat into resignation, she requested a meeting with library staff. She gathered allies, teachers, grandparents, and pastors, and together, they organized a public forum. She helped start a petition, appeared on local radio, and worked with the ACLU to better understand free speech protections. At the next board meeting, the room was full. Citizens spoke clearly: censorship does not reflect our values. Within weeks, the policy was reversed.

She wasn't a lawyer, organizer, or elected official. She was a parent, concerned that her kids would grow up with a narrower view of the world. What she demonstrated was not heroism, but **vigilance**. Democracy needs citizens like this, not just in national crises, but in local moments where freedom is quietly eroded unless someone objects.

II. Engage Your Local Democracy

The principles of vigilance take root locally. Engagement with town councils and school boards is how citizens convert democratic ideals into practical action.

National politics may dominate headlines, but democracy is lived, and most vulnerable, at the local level. It is in city councils, school boards, zoning commissions, and library boards that policies are shaped, budgets are allocated, and communities are defined. Vigilant citizens don't just vote; they show up where decisions are made.

Attend Local Government Meetings

City council sessions, planning boards, and budget hearings are often underattended, but decisions made there affect education, policing, housing, and climate resilience. These meetings are where democracy is practiced in its most immediate form. Public comment matters. Showing up shows that citizens are paying attention, which in turn can elevate accountability and broaden the conversation. Even observing the process builds understanding of how local governance operates and how decisions are shaped long before they reach the ballot box.

Join a Board or Commission

Most communities rely on volunteers to serve on advisory boards and committees. Whether you're helping allocate funding for the arts, overseeing historic preservation, or planning parks and trails, participation ensures democratic governance stays grounded in community values. Board service is also one of the most direct ways to influence local policy decisions and foster transparency, offering a front-row seat to how governance works and how it can be improved.

Know Your Local Officials

Accountability starts with familiarity. Know who represents you, not just in Congress, but on your school board, city council, county commission, and water district. Ask questions. Track their votes and public statements. Let them know you are paying attention and that you expect integrity and transparency. Developing relationships with local officials strengthens democratic feedback loops and reminds public servants that their constituents are informed, engaged, and invested.

Vote in Local Elections

Turnout for municipal and school board elections is often dismally low. Yet these are the contests that shape the institutions closest to your life, your schools, neighborhoods, and tax dollars. Local governments decide how streets are maintained, what books are in school libraries, and which public services receive funding. Ignoring these elections allows others to shape your daily environment unchecked. The vigilant citizen treats every election as consequential and makes local voting a civic habit, not an afterthought.

Run for Office

Representative democracy thrives when it draws from a wide range of lived experiences and community voices. Consider running for local office, school board, city council, or a commission seat. You don't need to be a political insider or policy expert. What democracy needs most is people rooted in their communities who are willing to serve with integrity, humility, and a commitment to the common good.

Benjamin Franklin famously remarked that the Constitution had created "a republic, if you can keep it." — Benjamin Franklin, remarks at the close of the Constitutional Convention, 1787 His point was simple: self-government depends on self-governors. Running for office is not just an act of ambition. It is a contribution to the maintenance of democratic life.

Local democracy is the training ground of national accountability. It is where the republic is either nourished or neglected.

From Frustration to Candidacy: A First-Time Campaign

In 2021, a high school science teacher named Rafael didn't plan to run for office. But when his district cut funding for civics programs and proposed new restrictions on teaching "controversial" topics, he realized that comment letters weren't enough. He filed paperwork to run for the local school board.

He had no campaign staff. No political experience. Just a sense that public education was worth defending.

Rafael spent evenings knocking on doors, handing out flyers at farmers' markets, and hosting town halls in living rooms. He didn't promise perfection; he promised transparency. "I'm not a politician," he told voters. "I'm a teacher who wants our kids to graduate prepared to think."

On Election Day, he won—by 238 votes.

As a board member, he helped block efforts to remove inclusive curricula, advocated for teacher protections, and pushed for better civic education funding. His campaign wasn't polished. But it was principled. He showed that running for office isn't about ambition, it's about ownership. When citizens see injustice, one option is to protest. Another is to **govern**.

Democracy needs both.

III. Defend Public Institutions

No matter how strong a constitution, democracy cannot function without institutions that support shared knowledge, justice, and reason. These are the bulwarks of a free society.

Institutions do not defend themselves. They require people, inside and outside, to preserve their integrity, purpose, and accessibility. In an age of ideological capture, budgetary neglect, and political pressure, public institutions like libraries, schools, the courts, and scientific agencies need vigilant defenders more than ever.

Support Local Libraries, Schools, and Public Media
These are the foundational spaces where democratic culture is cultivated. Advocate for their funding, resist censorship, and engage with them regularly. They are among the last remaining places committed to public knowledge and shared access. These institutions are not just buildings—they are civic sanctuaries that provide access to facts, foster critical thinking, and create spaces for dialogue across difference. Defending them is not charity, it is an investment in the infrastructure of a functioning democracy.

Champion Transparency and Accountability
Push for open meetings, public records, and ethical oversight in your local government. Demand clarity in budgeting and procurement processes. Participate in public comment periods. Support and protect whistleblowers who expose misconduct

or waste. Back independent audits and fact-based reporting. Sunshine laws exist for a reason; so use them. A transparent government is not a luxury of democracy; it is one of its most essential protections.

Push Back Against Ideological Censorship
From book bans to curriculum purges, the politicization of public institutions threatens their democratic function. Support educators, librarians, and administrators who resist partisan manipulation. Call out efforts to rewrite or erase history. Take concrete steps: sign petitions, attend public hearings, write letters to editors, and speak out on behalf of those targeted for defending intellectual freedom. Democracy depends on a full and honest reckoning with the past, and the courage to protect that truth in the present.

Speak Up for Truth-Based Institutions
Support local journalism, scientific agencies, and judicial independence. Defend their role as truth-tellers and fair arbiters in public life.

A democratic society is only as strong as the institutions that support public reason, education, and justice. When those are under attack, silence is complicity.

IV. Know and Use Your Rights

Awareness of rights is not enough; they must be exercised and defended in public life. Knowing how to act within the system makes democratic participation possible and powerful.

In a democracy, rights are not just protections. They are instruments of participation. Yet many citizens are unaware of the full range of civic tools at their disposal. Vigilant citizenship means knowing your rights, defending them when challenged, and using them to hold power accountable.

Vote in Every Election

Federal elections may draw more attention, but state, local, and even special elections often have more immediate impact on your community. These are the arenas where school curricula are shaped, policing policies are set, and infrastructure is funded or neglected. Every ballot is a chance to steer the direction of public life. Make a plan to vote—every time. Help others do the same. When participation falters, democracy weakens; when citizens show up, the system is strengthened from the ground up.

Understand the Constitution and Local Laws

The Constitution is not just a national symbol, it's a practical guide to your civic rights and responsibilities. Study it. Know what due process, equal protection, free speech, and checks and balances actually mean in practice. Explore your state constitution and local ordinances as well. Many of the rights and responsibilities that shape daily life originate at the local level. Understanding these frameworks empowers citizens to speak with confidence, advocate effectively, and challenge abuses of power when they arise.

Petition, Protest, and Participate

Democratic participation includes the right to peacefully assemble, advocate for change, and petition public officials. These aren't merely historical ideals, they are living tools for public accountability. Join rallies, sign and circulate petitions, submit public comments during rulemaking processes, and attend town halls. Know your local ordinances and your rights under the First Amendment. Teach others how to engage, too, because every civic action becomes a signal that democracy still matters.

Hold Power Accountable

Use open records laws to request public documents. Track campaign donations. Follow voting records. Show those in power that they are being watched, not with hostility, but with responsibility.

Knowing your rights is not enough. They must be used, defended, and extended to others. A right unexercised is a right easily eroded.

V. Build Coalitions, Not Echo Chambers

No one saves a democracy alone. Sustaining it requires alliances across difference, grounded in shared respect, common purpose, and a commitment to pluralism.

The strength of a democracy lies not in uniformity but in the ability of diverse people to work together across lines of difference. While partisan politics and social media often reward outrage and tribalism, vigilant citizens resist these pressures by building bridges, finding shared ground even with those they disagree with.

Work Across Lines of Difference
Seek out coalitions that unite people around common causes, clean water, school funding, public safety, housing, rather than partisan identity. Civic progress often begins with unlikely alliances.

Elevate Marginalized Voices
Healthy coalitions include those historically excluded from power. Make space at the table. Listen actively. Let leadership be shared. This means not just including different voices but actively removing barriers to participation, language access, scheduling, compensation, and recognition. Elevation also involves amplifying those perspectives in media, public forums, and policymaking spaces where they've long been ignored.

Practice Ideological Generosity
Not every disagreement is a threat to democracy. Assume good faith where possible. Engage disagreement as an opportunity to learn and sharpen ideas, not as a contest to be won. True ideological generosity means being willing to revise your own views in light of compelling evidence and principled argument. It means recognizing that persuasion is not domination, and that

the goal of public discourse is not to silence opposition, but to seek better answers together.

Invest in Relationships, Not Just Arguments

Democracy is more than ideas; it's people. Build trust. Volunteer together. Share meals. Lasting civic engagement is forged in human connection, not comment threads. Shared civic projects, like neighborhood cleanups, mutual aid drives, community gardens, or local history events, create bonds that transcend political differences and build coalitions rooted in shared purpose.

Resist the Urge to Vilify

In a pluralistic society, your fellow citizens will come from different parties, faiths, ethnicities, and traditions. Do not mistake difference for danger. Bipartisanship is not weakness. It is the hard work of building a functional democracy. When we demonize others for who they are or how they vote, we fracture the civic trust that democracy requires to function.

Citizenship is a team sport. Without coalitions grounded in shared purpose, even the best ideas will fail to move from ideal to policy.

VI. Teach the Next Generation

The future of the republic is shaped by what the next generation understands about its past, and what they believe about their power to shape its future.

A democracy without civic memory is a democracy at risk. The lessons of history, the principles of constitutional governance, and the habits of responsible citizenship must be passed forward, or they will be lost.

Model Civic Engagement

Children learn not just from books, but from behavior. Attend meetings. Discuss current events. Volunteer. Show them that civic duty is not abstract. It is a lived ethic. Involve them in the process, take them to vote, encourage them to attend public forums, and let them see how engagement looks in action. When children witness participation, especially at the local level, they internalize the message that democracy is something they can shape, not just inherit.

Advocate for Civic Education in Schools

Push for comprehensive, nonpartisan civics curricula that teach history honestly and encourage debate, inquiry, and responsibility. As President Ronald Reagan said in a 1988 address, "Since the founding of this Nation, education and democracy have gone hand in hand. Jefferson and the Founders believed a nation that governs itself, like ours, must rely upon an informed and engaged electorate." — Ronald Reagan, *Radio Address to the Nation on Education*, September 24, 1988 Civic education is not partisan. It is foundational.

Mentor and Empower Youth Leaders

Support young people in organizing, voting, speaking, and leading. Offer resources, encouragement, and space for their voices. The future is not theirs later, it is theirs now. Adults can mentor by coaching youth-led initiatives, helping them access civic networks and resources, or partnering on intergenerational projects that amplify youth leadership in real-world civic spaces.

Encourage Critical Thinking

Teach young people to question assumptions, seek truth, and defend their ideas with integrity. Democracy is not sustained by obedience, but by understanding.

The republic will be inherited by those who come next. Whether it survives in form only, or in both form and function, depends on what we teach them, intellectually, morally, and by example.

VII. Conclusion: Democracy Is Daily Work

To close, here is a summary of the practices that can help sustain our democracy every day: The habits of liberty are not sustained by sentiment or ceremony. They are kept alive through attention, effort, and resolve. If democracy is to survive the pressures of polarization, disinformation, and disengagement, it will be because enough citizens chose to do the unglamorous, persistent work of civic responsibility.

There is no single solution to democratic decay, only a constellation of choices, made by millions of people, every day. When you read carefully, listen generously, vote consistently, serve locally, speak up, and build bridges, you participate in the slow, necessary work of holding a republic together.

You do not need a title to serve the public. You do not need permission to defend truth. And you do not need to be fearless to be brave. You need only to care enough to act, and to act even when no one is watching.

As Shirley Chisholm once said, "Service is the rent we pay for the privilege of living on this earth." — Shirley Chisholm, *Unbought and Unbossed*, 1970 In a democracy, that rent is daily, and the lease is collective. The republic is not inherited intact. It is rebuilt, every generation, by those willing to serve.

A Citizen's Action Summary

- **Read widely. Think critically.**
  Learn from diverse sources and perspectives to better understand complex issues and avoid ideological bubbles.

- **Verify information before sharing it.**
  Check facts and sources before passing along news or claims, especially on social media.

- **Engage in respectful, principled dialogue.**
  Speak honestly, listen actively, and seek common ground

without sacrificing your values.

- **Attend public meetings. Get involved locally.**
Show up at school board, city council, or community events, where many important decisions are made.

- **Run for office—or support those who do.**
Consider stepping up to lead, or help candidates who reflect your values and priorities.

- **Vote in every election, especially local ones.**
Local elections often have the biggest impact on your daily life, don't sit them out.

- **Defend and strengthen public institutions.**
Support the systems that uphold democracy: courts, libraries, election boards, the free press, and more.

- **Exercise your rights—and teach others to do the same.**
Know your rights and freedoms, use them wisely, and help others understand theirs.

- **Build coalitions based on shared purpose, not partisan purity.**
Work with others across differences when values align. Progress requires collaboration, not division.

- **Support local journalism and independent media.**
A free, trusted press helps hold power accountable and ensures the public stays informed.

- **Ask better questions. Stay curious.**
In a polarized world, thoughtful inquiry is a powerful civic act, especially when done with humility and open-mindedness.

- **Recognize and support those who serve the public in good faith.**
  Federal employees, election workers, judges, and teachers are often unseen protectors of democracy. Acknowledge their role.

- **Pass on civic values to the next generation.**
  Share stories, teach the basics, and model engagement. Democracy only survives if it's taught, remembered, and lived.

These practices are not exhaustive. But they are essential.
This is how we hold the line, so we never have to say again: we gave it away.

Democracy does not collapse all at once. It corrodes in silence, when citizens look away, when institutions are left undefended, when voices go unheard. But the opposite is also true. Democracy can be restored, in classrooms, courtrooms, and communities, by people willing to show up. That is the quiet miracle of the republic: it is never finished, but it is always possible.

CHAPTER EIGHT

Civic Courage in Crisis — Case Studies in Vigilance

"The only thing necessary for the triumph of evil is for good people to do nothing." — Attributed to Edmund Burke

This chapter illustrates democracy in action through modern stories of civic courage. Each case study demonstrates the real-life significance of vigilance and moral clarity when democratic norms face direct threats.

Democracy often depends on ordinary people doing extraordinary things under pressure. While institutions matter and civic habits endure, it is the sudden, courageous choice to act, often alone, often quietly, that holds the line when democratic norms are under attack.

These are stories of **civic courage**. Modern case studies of people who refused to look away, refused to obey blindly, and refused to be silent. They remind us that vigilance is not just a theory. It is practiced. Often at great cost.

1. Lt. Col. Alexander Vindman: Upholding Constitutional Duty

In 2019, Lieutenant Colonel Alexander Vindman, a decorated Army officer and Ukraine expert serving on the National Security Council, listened to a phone call between President Donald Trump and Ukrainian President Volodymyr Zelensky. Disturbed by the content, which he perceived as an abuse of presidential power, Vindman reported his concerns through official channels.

His actions placed him at the center of a presidential impeachment inquiry. Despite facing political retaliation and personal attacks, Vindman testified publicly before Congress, emphasizing that his loyalty was to the Constitution above any individual leader. Addressing his father during his testimony, Vindman stated:

> "Dad, my sitting here today, in the U.S. Capitol talking to our elected officials is proof that you made the right decision forty years ago to leave the Soviet Union and come here to the United States of America in search of a better life for our family. Do not worry. I will be fine for telling the truth."
> — *Lt. Col. Alexander Vindman, Congressional Testimony, November 19, 2019*

Vindman's courage highlighted the importance of accountability and the role of public servants in safeguarding democratic principles.

2. Frances Haugen: Exposing the Impact of Algorithms

In 2021, Frances Haugen, a former product manager at Facebook, disclosed thousands of internal documents revealing that the company's algorithms prioritized engagement, even when it led to the spread of misinformation and harm to users' mental health.

She testified before Congress, asserting that Facebook consistently chose profit over public safety. In her testimony, Haugen stated:

> "The choices being made inside of Facebook are disastrous—for our children, for our public safety, for our privacy and for our democracy."
> — *Frances Haugen, Senate Testimony, October 5, 2021*

Haugen's revelations sparked widespread discussions about the ethical responsibilities of tech companies and the need for greater transparency. Her actions underscored the significance of whistleblowers in holding powerful institutions accountable in the digital age.

3. Shaye Moss and Ruby Freeman: Defending Electoral Integrity

During the 2020 U.S. presidential election, Georgia election workers Shaye Moss and her mother, Ruby Freeman, became targets of false conspiracy theories alleging voter fraud. These unfounded accusations led to severe harassment, including death threats and racist abuse.

Despite the personal toll, both women remained committed to their roles in ensuring a fair electoral process. In her testimony before the House Select Committee, Moss recounted:

> "I felt horrible. I felt like it was all my fault. Like if I would have never decided to be an elections worker, like, I could have done anything else, but that's what I decided to do. And now people are lying and spreading rumors and lies and attacking my mom. I felt horrible for picking this job and being the one that always wants to help and always there, never missing not one election. I just felt like it was my fault for putting my family in this situation."
> — *Shaye Moss, House Select Committee Testimony, June 21, 2022*

Their experiences brought national attention to the vulnerabilities faced by election workers and the importance of protecting those who uphold democratic systems.

4. Masha Gessen: Chronicling the Rise of Autocracy

Journalist and author Masha Gessen has extensively documented the mechanisms of authoritarian regimes, drawing parallels between developments in Russia and emerging trends in the United States. Through works like "Surviving Autocracy," Gessen has provided insights into how democratic institutions can erode under autocratic pressures. In their writing, Gessen observed:

> "It is difficult to accept that the country you live in is becoming less free—but it is fatal to ignore it."
> — *Masha Gessen, "Autocracy: Rules for Survival," The New York Review of Books, November 10, 2016*

Their writings serve as a warning and a guide, emphasizing the need for vigilance and active participation in democratic processes. Gessen's work exemplifies the role of journalism in preserving civic awareness and resisting authoritarianism.

Conclusion: Courage Is Contagious

These stories span continents and professions. They differ in scope, background, and context. But they are united by a common ethic: **truth matters, process matters, democracy matters**.

Not every citizen will face a microphone, a courtroom, or a smear campaign. But every citizen will face a moment when doing nothing feels easier than doing the right thing.

Vigilance, at its core, is a choice. And as these individuals show, **that choice is the beginning of preservation**.

CONCLUSION

No Longer Quiet.

A Citizen's Guide to Protecting Our Democracy

Democracy is not a static achievement but a dynamic obligation. The authors surveyed across these chapters warn that liberty is neither self-sustaining nor self-correcting. From ancient Athens to the digital age, their message remains clear:

A democracy that does not educate its citizens to question, engage, and dissent is a democracy that will not survive.

The republic endures only if its citizens remain vigilant.

In the pages before, we traced democracy's philosophical roots, examined its fictional warnings, analyzed its historical unraveling, explored the erosion of civic institutions, and honored the individuals who stand as its last line of defense.

This vigilance is not the domain of the few, but the duty of the many. It manifests in classrooms and courthouses, libraries and lunch counters, newsrooms and neighborhood councils. It is sustained by the hard work of learning, listening, debating, organizing, and voting. It requires citizens who are not only informed but empowered, who see freedom not as a personal entitlement but as a public responsibility.

Behind every law, policy, and democratic safeguard stand individuals, federal workers, attorneys, whistleblowers, educators, activists, and everyday citizens, who refuse to let principle collapse under pressure. These are the unsung stewards of democracy who choose conscience over complacency and act in defense of the public good even when no spotlight shines. They are the living infrastructure of the republic, and their actions often make the difference between resilience and ruin.

From the park ranger to the public defender, the government analyst to the grassroots organizer, the democratic experiment depends on those willing to show up, speak out, and hold the line. Their work proves that democracy does not merely reside in documents or elections. It lives in the daily decisions of people who understand their roles as caretakers of something far bigger than themselves.

Throughout this book, we have drawn upon thinkers, writers, and movements that understood democracy to be a living system, fragile, fallible, but always capable of renewal through the actions of committed individuals. From the philosophers of antiquity to the dissidents of totalitarian regimes, from the literary seers to the modern reformers, the message resounds: democratic collapse is not inevitable, but neither is democratic survival.

The future of the republic does not depend on heroic leaders or perfect institutions. It depends on us, on our capacity to discern truth from noise, to value education over indoctrination, and to practice civic life with courage and clarity. We must demand more of our schools, our media, and ourselves.

If democracy fails, it will not be because the people lacked power.

It will be because they surrendered it, slowly, passively, and often unknowingly. But if democracy endures, it will be because citizens remembered what it requires: participation, principled dissent, and a refusal to abandon the public square.

To that end, we must teach. We must read. We must argue. We must hope. We must serve. We must resist. We must remember that democracy is not kept alive by belief, but by action. And above all, we must remain vigilant, because in the end, the survival of the republic depends not just on laws, but on its most vital infrastructure: a vigilant citizenry. Ultimately, democracy survives not by accident but by intention, through millions of quiet acts of vigilance by everyday people who choose to show up, speak out, and hold the line.

> "The price of freedom is eternal vigilance." — Attributed to Thomas Jefferson, commonly cited in American civic discourse

APPENDIX A: SOURCES

Annotated Bibliography of Sources

E ach work cited in this book contributed uniquely to the central thesis. Below is a list of sources cited along with a brief explanation of their relevance to the argument of democratic preservation.

Albright, Horace. Quoted in Creating the National Park Service: The Missing Years, by Horace M. Albright and Marian Albright Schenck. Norman: University of Oklahoma Press, 1999. — A vivid depiction of the role of federal rangers, this quote highlights the selfless public service ethos central to democratic stewardship.

Arendt, Hannah. *The Origins of Totalitarianism*. New York: Harcourt, Brace, 1951. — A foundational work exploring how truth and reason are dismantled under totalitarian regimes, providing a critical lens for understanding democratic fragility.

Asimov, Isaac. "A Cult of Ignorance." *Newsweek*, January 21, 1980. — A prescient essay warning of the dangers of anti-intellectualism and its corrosive effects on democratic culture and public discourse.

Atwood, Margaret. *The Handmaid's Tale*. Toronto: McClelland and Stewart, 1985. — A dystopian novel that illustrates how authoritarianism can emerge through cultural nostalgia and selective memory, especially regarding women's rights.

Bradbury, Ray. *Fahrenheit 451*. New York: Ballantine Books, 1953. — Explores voluntary censorship and the societal collapse that follows mass disengagement from reading, learning, and critical thinking.

Brandeis, Louis. Quoted in Philippa Strum, *Louis D. Brandeis: Justice for the People*. Cambridge, MA: Harvard University Press, 1984. — Highlights the foundational belief that democracy requires morally grounded and well-informed citizens.

Bullard, Robert D. *Dumping in Dixie: Race, Class, and Environmental Quality*. Boulder, CO: Westview Press, 1990. — Documents the environmental injustices faced by marginalized communities, highlighting systemic civic exclusion and democratic inequality.

Carson, Rachel. *Silent Spring*. Boston: Houghton Mifflin, 1962. — A pioneering work of environmental science that also critiques the suppression of scientific truth in public policy—a central concern in democratic integrity.

Chisholm, Shirley. *Unbought and Unbossed*. Boston: Houghton Mifflin, 1970. — Civil rights leader and congresswoman. Her quote about public service as "the rent we pay" emphasizes everyday democratic duty.

Chomsky, Noam. "The Responsibility of Intellectuals." *The New York Review of Books*, February 23, 1967. — Challenges the educated class to expose propaganda and uphold truth in public life, emphasizing their role in sustaining democratic discourse.

Davis, Angela Y. *Freedom Is a Constant Struggle: Ferguson, Palestine, and the Foundations of a Movement*. Chicago: Haymarket Books, 2016. — Connects global struggles for justice, underlining the need for activism and transnational solidarity in defending democratic ideals.

Douglass, Frederick. "What to the Slave Is the Fourth of July?" Speech, Rochester, NY, July 5, 1852. — A searing critique of

American hypocrisy, emphasizing the gap between democratic ideals and lived reality, especially for marginalized populations.

Franklin, Benjamin. Remarks at the Constitutional Convention, 1787. In *The Records of the Federal Convention of 1787*, edited by Max Farrand. New Haven: Yale University Press, 1911. — Famously said, "A republic, if you can keep it," summarizing the conditional nature of self-government. Underscores the ongoing civic work required to preserve democracy.

Gessen, Masha. 2016. "Autocracy: Rules for Survival." *The New York Review of Books*, November 10, 2016. https://www.nybooks.com/online/2016/11/10/trump-election-autocracy-rules-for-survival/

Ginsberg, Allen. *Howl*. San Francisco: City Lights Books, 1956. — A defining poem of postwar American literature, Ginsberg's work warns of cultural and intellectual decay, resonating with themes of disengagement and societal erosion.

Haugen, Frances. 2021. *Testimony Before the U.S. Senate Committee on Commerce, Science, and Transportation*, October 5, 2021. https://www.npr.org/2021/10/05/1043194385/whistleblowers-testimony-facebook-instagram

Hitchens, Christopher. *Letters to a Young Contrarian*. New York: Basic Books, 2001. — A call to principled dissent as a civic virtue, reminding readers that opposition and nonconformity are essential to democratic resilience.

Huxley, Aldous. *Brave New World*. London: Chatto & Windus, 1932. — Warns of a future where freedom is surrendered not through coercion but through comfort and distraction—paralleling current threats to public engagement.

Jackson, Robert H. *Terminiello v. City of Chicago*, 337 U.S. 1 (1949), dissenting opinion. — Provides the foundational quote, "The Constitution is not a suicide pact," emphasizing the balance between liberty and public order within constitutional boundaries.

Jefferson, Thomas. Letter to Colonel Charles Yancey, January 6, 1816. — Reinforces Jefferson's enduring concern that freedom and ignorance are incompatible, highlighting the necessity of an educated citizenry in a functioning democracy.

Jefferson, Thomas. Attributed. "The price of freedom is eternal vigilance." Often cited in civic discourse to emphasize the ongoing responsibility of citizens to safeguard liberty. While the exact origin is debated, the sentiment reflects Jeffersonian principles of participatory government.

Kerouac, Jack. *On the Road*. New York: Viking Press, 1957. — A novel that celebrates individual freedom and questions conformity, Kerouac's voice challenges readers to value liberty over comfort and mediocrity.

Levitsky, Steven, and Daniel Ziblatt. *How Democracies Die*. New York: Crown Publishing Group, 2018. — A contemporary political analysis showing how democratic erosion often occurs gradually through the manipulation of norms and institutions.

Lewis, Sinclair. *It Can't Happen Here*. New York: Doubleday, Doran & Company, 1935. — A satirical novel that explores how authoritarianism can rise in America through populism, passivity, and institutional decay.

Lincoln, Abraham. "The Perpetuation of Our Political Institutions." Speech, Springfield, IL, January 27, 1838. — Warns of internal threats to the republic, calling for a national culture of legal fidelity and civic vigilance.

Madison, James. *Federalist No. 10*, in *The Federalist Papers*. New York: New American Library, 1961. — A foundational text on the dangers of factionalism and the necessity of enlightened public opinion in sustaining republican government.

Madison, James. Letter to W. T. Barry, August 4, 1822. — Argues that popular government requires informed citizens, asserting that knowledge is the only guardian of true liberty.

Marshall, Thurgood. Quoted in Juan Williams, *Thurgood Marshall: American Revolutionary*. New York: Crown Publishers, 1998. — Reinforces the moral imperative of civic action by every citizen in defending democracy from injustice and inequality.

Mill, John Stuart. *On Liberty*. London: John W. Parker and Son, 1859. — Defends free expression and intellectual diversity as essential pillars of democratic society and individual autonomy.

Moss, Shaye. 2022. *Testimony Before the U.S. House Select Committee to Investigate the January 6th Attack on the United States Capitol*, June 21, 2022. https://www.npr.org/2022/06/22/1106459556/shaye-moss-staffed-an-election-office-in-georgia-then-she-was-targeted-by-trump

Orwell, George. *1984*. London: Secker & Warburg, 1949. — A dystopian masterpiece that explores the consequences of state surveillance, historical revisionism, and the destruction of objective truth.

Plato. *The Republic*. Translated by G. M. A. Grube. Revised by C. D. C. Reeve. Indianapolis: Hackett Publishing Company, 1992. — Philosophically examines justice and the structure of the ideal state, including the dangers of democratic excess and the descent into tyranny.

Postman, Neil. *Amusing Ourselves to Death: Public Discourse in the Age of Show Business*. New York: Viking Penguin, 1985. — Analyzes how television and entertainment-driven media undermine rational public debate, weakening the foundation of informed democracy.

Powell, Colin. Quoted in "8 Favorite Quotes About Government Workers." GovLoop. Accessed [insert date]. https://www.govloop.com/8-favorite-quotes-about-government — Underscores the importance of talent, integrity, and individual dedication within public institutions as the key to democratic success.

Reagan, Ronald. "Radio Address to the Nation on Education." September 24, 1988. Ronald Reagan Presidential Library. — Advocates for civic education and an informed electorate, framing education as foundational to democratic survival.

Roberts, John. *National Federation of Independent Business v. Sebelius*, 567 U.S. 519 (2012). — Quoted in this book for his reminder that while the Constitution empowers the federal government, it also restrains it, underscoring the importance of constitutional boundaries in a healthy republic.

Roosevelt, Theodore. "Citizenship in a Republic" speech, delivered at the Sorbonne, Paris, April 23, 1910. Reprinted in *The Strenuous Life: Essays and Addresses*. New York: The Century Co., 1900. — Emphasizes personal responsibility and the active role of every citizen in maintaining and defending the democratic republic.

Sams, Charles F. "Chuck," III. Remarks at "Consider This: The Lands We Live On with Chuck Sams," Town Hall Presentation. Oregon Humanities, Pendleton Center for the Arts, Pendleton, OR, April 9, 2025.

Thompson, Hunter S. *The Proud Highway: Saga of a Desperate Southern Gentleman*. New York: Ballantine Books, 1997. — A collection of letters from the author's early years, including reflections on civic duty, apathy, and the fragility of American freedom.

Tocqueville, Alexis de. *Democracy in America*. Translated by Harvey C. Mansfield and Delba Winthrop. Chicago: University of Chicago Press, 2000. — Offers foundational insights on the character of American civic life, particularly the power and responsibility of individual citizens within democratic institutions.

Vindman, Alexander. 2019. *Testimony Before the U.S. House Intelligence Committee*, November 19, 2019. https://

www.npr.org/2021/08/10/1026395534/alexander-vindman-key-witness-to-trump-impeachment-shares-his-american-story

Washington, George. *Farewell Address*, September 19, 1796. — Urges national unity, warns against factionalism, and champions public education as a safeguard of liberty. Serves as both a political and moral guide for future generations.

Washington, George. *First Inaugural Address*, April 30, 1789. — Declares that the sacred fire of liberty is entrusted to the American people, emphasizing their direct responsibility in maintaining a free government.

Wright, Richard. "The Man Who Was Almost a Man." In *Eight Men*. New York: Harper & Brothers, 1961. — A short story that critiques systemic disenfranchisement and the symbolic dimensions of rebellion in marginalized communities.

APPENDIX B:
FURTHER READING

Recommended Reading
for Civic Literacy

Accessible books to inform, inspire, and empower democratic engagement:

Bowling Alone: The Collapse and Revival of American Community — *Robert Putnam*
Explores how declining civic and social engagement threatens democracy and what we can do to rebuild community bonds.

Democracy Awakening — *Heather Cox Richardson*
A concise, compelling overview of how American democracy has been shaped, and challenged, over time, designed for general audiences.

Democracy in Retrograde — *Emily Amick and Sami Sage*
A modern, practical guide to civic engagement and activism for those feeling disillusioned by politics and media.

Hope for Democracy: How Citizens Can Bring Reason Back into Politics — *John Gastil and Katherine Knobloch*
Demonstrates how inclusive and reasoned public participation

can rebuild trust and strengthen democratic institutions.

March (Trilogy) — *John Lewis, Andrew Aydin, and Nate Powell*
A graphic memoir chronicling the life of civil rights icon John Lewis and the grassroots power of civic movements.

Not for Profit: Why Democracy Needs the Humanities — *Martha Nussbaum*
Argues that arts and humanities education is essential for critical thinking, empathy, and civic responsibility.

On Democracy — *Robert A. Dahl*
A foundational introduction to democratic theory and why democracy matters—clear, brief, and readable.

On Tyranny: Twenty Lessons from the Twentieth Century — *Timothy Snyder*
A small but urgent handbook of historical lessons and modern warnings for protecting democracy.

Power to the People — *Danny Sriskandarajah*
Explores how participatory democracy and collective action can counter democratic erosion and inequality.

Silent Spring — *Rachel Carson*
A groundbreaking book that sparked the environmental movement and highlighted the role of informed public advocacy.

Talking to Strangers: Anxieties of Citizenship since Brown v. Board of Education — *Danielle Allen*
Explores the challenges of civic trust and inclusion in the face of racial injustice.

Teaching to Transgress: Education as the Practice of Freedom — *bell hooks*
Blends memoir and philosophy to advocate for liberatory education and democratic empowerment through learning.

The Civic Bargain: How Democracy Survives — *Brook Manville and Josiah Ober*

Makes the case for renewing the foundational agreements and relationships that hold democratic societies together.

Unrig: How to Fix Our Broken Democracy — *Daniel G. Newman and George O'Connor*
A graphic novel that clearly explains structural reforms and how citizens can make democracy more responsive.

Young People, Citizenship and Political Participation: Combating Civic Deficit? — *Jean-Paul Gagnon et al.*
Focuses on youth civic engagement and educational strategies for developing lifelong democratic participation.

Here is a list of more formal civics, philosophy, and political books for further exploration:

A Time to Build — *Yuval Levin*
Examines the decline of trust in American institutions and offers a case for rebuilding civic and social responsibility.

Between the World and Me — *Ta-Nehisi Coates*
A deeply personal reflection on race, identity, and the American democratic promise, written as a letter to the author's son.

Democracy in America — *Alexis de Tocqueville*
A seminal analysis of American civic life, exploring the relationship between liberty, equality, and participatory

democracy.

Democratic Education and the Public Sphere — *Danielle S. Allen and Rob Reich, eds.*
A collection of essays exploring how education and civic spaces can support democratic engagement.

Democracy and Education — *John Dewey*
A classic argument that democratic citizenship must be cultivated through public education, critical inquiry, and ethical reasoning.

Development as Freedom — *Amartya Sen*
Presents the argument that economic and political freedoms are mutually reinforcing and essential to human development.

Dumping in Dixie: Race, Class, and Environmental Quality — *Robert D. Bullard*
Analyzes environmental injustice and the civic marginalization of vulnerable communities.

Hope for Democracy: How Citizens Can Bring Reason Back into Politics — *John Gastil and Katherine Knobloch*
Demonstrates how inclusive and reasoned public participation can rebuild trust and strengthen democratic institutions.

How the South Won the Civil War — *Heather Cox Richardson*
A political history exploring how the ideals of oligarchy and white supremacy continued to shape American institutions well beyond the Civil War.

Two Treatises of Government — *John Locke*
A philosophical foundation for democratic governance and the idea that government is legitimate only when it protects natural rights and operates with the consent of the governed.

APPENDIX C: QUESTIONS

*Classroom and Book Club
Discussion Questions*

1. **Which warning in the book feels most relevant today? Why?**

2. **How do the fictional depictions of dystopias compare with real-world examples of democratic decline?**

3. **What role should education play in shaping a democratic citizen?**

4. **Do you believe media literacy should be taught alongside civics? Why or why not?**

5. **Which authors or thinkers in the book challenged your assumptions the most?**

6. **How might civic education be reimagined to meet the challenges of the digital age?**

7. **Is apathy as dangerous as malice in a democracy? Why?**

8. **What is the difference between patriotism and**

nationalism, and how does it impact democratic resilience?

9. Should intellectual dissent always be protected—even when it's unpopular or uncomfortable?

10. How do we balance comfort and liberty in a consumer society?

11. What does it mean to "give democracy away," and have you seen this dynamic in your own community?

12. How can everyday citizens and residents hold the line against institutional failure or democratic erosion?

13. Which part of the book inspired you to take action—or reconsider your civic responsibilities?

14. What are the small, everyday actions that build civic trust or restore public institutions?

15. How can stories—fictional or historical—be used as tools for democratic renewal?

16. What responsibilities do citizens have in moments of disinformation, polarization, or crisis?

17. Can a democracy function without shared facts? What happens when consensus breaks down?

18. How might trust be rebuilt between government and the people it serves?

APPENDIX D: GLOSSARY

Glossary and Important
Terms/Concepts

Activism — Efforts by individuals or groups to bring about social or political change, often through protests, petitions, advocacy campaigns, lobbying, or digital organizing. Activism is a key form of collective action and serves as a mechanism for citizens to influence public policy, challenge injustice, and amplify underrepresented voices in a democracy.

Algorithmic Bias — Systematic and unintended discrimination that results from algorithms processing data in ways that reflect or amplify existing social biases. In civic life, algorithmic bias can distort public discourse, access to information, and the visibility of political viewpoints.

Authoritarianism — A system of governance characterized by strong central power and limited political freedoms, often marked by the absence of democratic institutions and the suppression of dissent.

Bipartisanship — Cooperation or collaboration between members of different political parties, especially in the legislative process. Bipartisanship is often viewed as essential for passing durable, widely supported laws and for maintaining the stability of democratic institutions. While it requires compromise and mutual respect, it can be difficult to achieve in highly polarized environments.

Censorship — The suppression or prohibition of speech, writing, or information considered objectionable or dangerous by authorities.

Checks and Balances — A foundational principle of constitutional democracy in which each branch of government (executive, legislative, judicial) has the authority to limit the powers of the other branches. Checks and balances are designed to prevent any one branch from becoming too powerful and to safeguard against tyranny.

Civic Duty — The responsibilities and obligations individuals have as members of a democratic society, such as voting, staying informed, serving on a jury, respecting the law, and engaging in civil discourse. Fulfilling one's civic duty is essential to maintaining democratic institutions and collective self-governance.

Civic Engagement — The participation of individuals in political or community activities intended to influence public policy, solve problems, or strengthen democratic society. This includes voting, attending public meetings, advocacy, volunteering, and civil discourse.

Civic Literacy — The knowledge and skills needed to participate effectively in civic life, including understanding governmental processes, rights, responsibilities, and the importance of informed engagement.

Civil Disobedience — The nonviolent refusal to obey laws or governmental policies as a form of protest, often undertaken to highlight injustice and advocate for change. It has played a central role in democratic movements around the world.

Collective Action — Coordinated efforts by a group of individuals working together to achieve a shared goal or advance a common interest. In a democratic context, collective action often takes the form of voting, organizing, protesting, volunteering, or advocating for policy change. It reflects the principle that while individual voices matter, meaningful change often requires collaboration, solidarity, and sustained civic engagement.

Communism — A political and economic ideology advocating for a classless society in which property and the means of production are communally owned, and each individual contributes and receives according to their ability and needs.

Conservatism — A political philosophy emphasizing tradition, social stability, limited government, individual responsibility, and the preservation of established institutions. Philosophical conservatism prioritizes gradual change, skepticism of concentrated power, and a respect for cultural and moral order.

Constituency — The group of people represented by an elected official. Constituents typically live in a defined geographic area and rely on their representative to advocate for their interests in legislative or governmental bodies.

Constitutional Crisis — A situation in which the structures, rules, or norms defined by a constitution are challenged, ignored, or unable to resolve major conflicts between branches of government. Constitutional crises can undermine public trust, trigger instability, and threaten the integrity of democratic governance.

Crisis of Legitimacy — A loss of public confidence in a government, institution, or system's right to exercise authority. When large portions of the population question the fairness, effectiveness, or representativeness of those in power, a legitimacy crisis can lead to unrest, disengagement, or demands for reform.

Democracy — A form of government in which power resides with the people, who exercise it either directly or through elected representatives, based on principles of majority rule, political equality, and individual rights.

Democratic Legitimacy — The idea that a government is justified and rightful only when it is accountable to its people and reflects their will through fair, transparent, and participatory processes. Democracy is valued not only for its structure, but for its moral foundation: that all people are equal, all voices matter, and power must answer to the public it serves.

Democratic Republic — A government system combining elements of democracy (elected representatives, rule of law) with republican structures (a constitution limiting majority power and protecting minority rights).

Disinformation — Deliberately false or misleading information spread to deceive or manipulate public opinion.

Due Process — The legal principle that guarantees individuals fair treatment through the normal judicial system, including the right to a fair trial, notice of legal action, and an opportunity to be heard. Due process protects against arbitrary government action and is a cornerstone of the rule of law.

Echo Chamber — A media or social environment in which people are only exposed to information or opinions that reinforce their existing beliefs, often leading to increased polarization and reduced critical engagement with opposing views.

Fascism — An authoritarian and nationalistic system of government and social organization characterized by dictatorial power, forcible suppression of opposition, and strong regimentation of society and the economy.

Filibuster — A procedural tactic used in some legislative bodies, especially the U.S. Senate, to delay or block action on a bill by extending debate indefinitely. While intended as a tool for minority voices, it has also been criticized for obstructing democratic decision-making.

Freedom of Assembly — The right of individuals to gather peacefully for protest, celebration, or collective action. It is a cornerstone of democratic life and protected in many constitutions, including the First Amendment of the U.S. Constitution.

Freedom of Speech — The right to express opinions and ideas without government interference or regulation, protected in democratic societies but often restricted under authoritarian regimes.

Freedom of the Press — The right of journalists and media organizations to publish information and opinions without government censorship. A free press plays a vital role in exposing corruption, informing the public, and holding power accountable.

Gerrymandering — The deliberate manipulation of electoral district boundaries to give one political party or group an unfair advantage, often undermining the principle of fair representation.

Grassroots Movement — A political or social movement driven by everyday people at the local or community level, rather than by centralized or elite organizations. Grassroots movements often rely on collective action, local engagement, and bottom-up pressure to advocate for change.

Incumbent — A person currently holding a particular political office. Incumbents often have advantages in elections due to name recognition, existing support networks, and access to resources.

Judicial Review — The power of courts to assess whether a law, policy, or executive action is consistent with the Constitution. In the United States, this principle was established in *Marbury v. Madison* (1803) and gives the judiciary a key role in balancing government power.

Although **Article III of the Constitution** does not explicitly mention judicial review, it grants the judicial branch authority over all cases "arising under this Constitution," which the Supreme Court interpreted as including the power to invalidate laws that conflict with constitutional principles. Chief Justice John Marshall's opinion in *Marbury* argued that it is the duty of the judiciary to "say what the law is," and that enforcing unconstitutional laws would violate both the Constitution and the rule of law.

Liberalism — A political philosophy grounded in the principles of individual liberty, equality, rule of law, and representative government. Classical liberalism emphasizes civil rights and free markets, while modern liberalism often includes a role for government in promoting social justice and economic opportunity.

Libertarianism — A political philosophy that prioritizes individual freedom, minimal government intervention, and free-market principles. Libertarians generally advocate for strong personal and economic liberties, often emphasizing voluntary association and skepticism of state power.

Lobbying — The practice of attempting to influence elected officials or government decisions on behalf of individuals, organizations, or interest groups. While a legal and common part of democratic systems, lobbying can raise concerns about unequal access and influence in policymaking.

Majority Rule / Minority Rights — A foundational concept in democracy that balances the will of the majority with protections for individuals and groups in the minority. This principle ensures that while decisions are made through majority consensus, fundamental rights and liberties are not subject to popular vote.

Misinformation — Incorrect or misleading information shared without the intent to deceive. Unlike disinformation, misinformation is often spread unknowingly but can still have serious consequences for public understanding.

Nationalism — A political ideology centered on national identity and sovereignty, which can foster unity but may also lead to exclusionary or authoritarian tendencies.

Nonviolent Resistance — A strategic approach to protest and change that rejects violence in favor of peaceful methods such as marches, civil disobedience, boycotts, and symbolic acts. Nonviolent resistance has been a powerful force in democratic and human rights movements around the world.

Partisanship — Strong allegiance to a political party, often leading to a reluctance to compromise, increased polarization, and a weakening of shared civic norms.

Pluralism — A belief in and commitment to a society where multiple groups, identities, and perspectives coexist and are respected within a shared political system. Pluralism values diversity, dialogue, and peaceful disagreement as strengths of democratic life.

Polarization — The process by which political attitudes and identities become more extreme and oppositional, often reducing the ability of people to find common ground or engage in meaningful dialogue.

Populism — A political approach that claims to represent the common people, often characterized by distrust of elites and institutions, and in some cases, by the oversimplification of complex issues.

Propaganda — Information, especially biased or misleading, used to promote a political cause or ideology.

Public Institution — An organization established and maintained by government to serve the public good, such as schools, libraries, courts, election boards, and public health agencies. Trust in these institutions is essential to the functioning of democracy.

Ranked-Choice Voting — An electoral system in which voters rank candidates in order of preference. If no candidate wins a majority of first-choice votes, the lowest-ranked candidates are eliminated and their votes redistributed, until a candidate achieves a majority. It is designed to reflect broader voter preferences and reduce strategic voting.

Republic — A form of government in which the country is considered a public matter (*res publica*), and officials are accountable to the people and operate under a constitution or set of laws. In the United States, representatives are elected locally to represent their constituents at all levels of government.

Rule of Law — The principle that all individuals and institutions are subject to and accountable under the law, applied equally and fairly.

Separation of Powers — A system of governance in which the executive, legislative, and judicial branches operate independently to prevent any one branch from consolidating too much power. It is a foundational principle of constitutional democracies, designed to protect liberty and ensure checks and balances.

Social Contract — A philosophical concept that individuals consent to form a society and accept certain rules and responsibilities in exchange for protection of their rights and freedoms. It is a foundational idea in democratic theory, especially as articulated by thinkers like Locke, Rousseau, and Hobbes.

Socialism — A political and economic system advocating collective or governmental ownership and administration of the means of production and distribution of goods, typically aiming to reduce inequality.

Tyranny — Oppressive and unjust government or rule, often by a single ruler or a small group, characterized by the abuse of power and the denial of individual freedoms.

Voter Suppression — Any action or policy that makes it harder for eligible citizens to vote, including restrictive ID laws, purging of voter rolls, limited polling places, or misinformation about election procedures.

THE UNITED STATES SYSTEM OF GOVERNMENT

In the United States, the Constitution establishes a separation of powers among three co-equal branches of government: the legislative, executive, and judicial. This system was designed to prevent the concentration of power and to ensure that each branch can check and balance the others. Together, they uphold the rule of law, safeguard individual rights, and ensure that no single authority dominates the democratic process.

Legislative Branch

Makes the laws.

The legislative branch consists of Congress, which is divided into two chambers: the House of Representatives and the Senate. Congress has the power to draft, debate, and pass laws; approve budgets; declare war; and conduct oversight of the executive branch. It represents the people and the states in policymaking and plays a central role in democratic accountability.

Executive Branch

Enforces the laws.

The executive branch is led by the President, who serves as both the head of state and commander-in-chief of the armed forces. The executive includes the Vice President, the President's Cabinet, and numerous federal agencies that implement and administer laws passed by Congress. This branch ensures that laws are carried out and manages foreign affairs, national defense, and executive policy.

Judicial Branch

Interprets the laws.

The judicial branch consists of the federal court system, with the Supreme Court at its head. Courts have the power to interpret laws and the Constitution, resolve legal disputes, and review the constitutionality of laws and executive actions. This branch serves as a guardian of rights and a check on the other two branches through judicial review.

Together, these three branches are designed to operate independently while maintaining a system of checks and balances. This structure protects against tyranny, reinforces accountability, and ensures that power in a democratic republic is distributed and not concentrated.

ABOUT THE AUTHOR

D.c Burnette

D.C Burnette is a multidisciplinary writer, attorney, and public servant whose work lives at the intersection of civic life, preservation, and democratic practice. With a voice shaped by decades of public service and a lens honed through education, law, and civic duty, he writes to remind us that democracy is not self-sustaining. It is something we build, question, defend, and pass on.

Before publishing, D.C. Burnette spent years working across sectors, as a public servant, organizational strategist, policy advisor, and interpreter of landscapes, helping communities navigate the tension between institutional power and public voice. He has taught civics in classrooms, drafted policy in federal offices, and developed plans that helped everyday people make sense of complex systems. His experience spans courtrooms and community meetings, trailheads and town halls; always rooted in a belief that civic literacy is a form of resilience. Whether walking students through the Constitution, guiding hikers through protected lands, saving historic buildings for re-use, or designing campaigns that translate law into language, He has spent a lifetime turning democratic theory into practice.

Mr. Burnette's work is published through El Burno Publishing, the public-interest imprint of El Burno Productions, Ltd.